Congressmen, Constituents, and Contributors

STUDIES IN PUBLIC CHOICE

Gordon Tullock, *Editor*
Virginia Polytechnic Institute and State University

Other volumes in the series:

James M. Buchanan and Richard E. Wagner, *Fiscal Responsibility in Constitutional Democracy,* 1978

Richard B. McKenzie, *The Political Economy of the Educational Process,* 1979

Richard D. Auster and Morris Silver, *The State as a Firm,* 1979

This series, like the journal *Public Choice,* is devoted to an important aspect of the interaction between the disciplines of economics and political science: the application of economic methods of analysis to matters that have traditionally been political. The objective of these publications is to further the growth of knowledge in this intersection of the social sciences.

Congressmen, Constituents, and Contributors

Determinants of Roll Call Voting in the House of Representatives

JAMES B. KAU

PAUL H. RUBIN

The University of Georgia

WITH CONTRIBUTIONS FROM

R. CARTER HILL

DONALD C. KEENAN

MARTINUS NIJHOFF PUBLISHING

BOSTON/THE HAGUE/LONDON

DISTRIBUTORS FOR NORTH AMERICA:
Martinus Nijhoff Publishing
Kluwer Boston, Inc.
190 Old Derby Street
Hingham, Massachusetts 02043, U.S.A.

DISTRIBUTORS OUTSIDE NORTH AMERICA:
Kluwer Academic Publishers Group
Distribution Centre
P.O. Box 322
3300 AH Dordrecht, The Netherlands

Library of Congress Cataloging in Publication Data

Kau, James B.
    Congressmen, constituents, and contributors.

    (Studies in public choice; #4)
    Includes index.
    1. United States. Congress. House—Voting.
2. Elections—United States—Campaign funds.
I. Rubin, Paul H. II. Title. III. Series.
JK1319.K38   328.73'0775   81-4979

ISBN 0-89838-070-7   AACR2

Printed in the United States of America

CONTENTS

v

ACKNOWLEDGMENTS

This book represents the culmination of a research effort that went on for several years. Over that time many people had helpful comments on this research. Not all of these people agreed with all of the results. We would, however, like to thank them in any case. Those who have helped with their comments are: Yoram Barzel, Thomas Borcherding, Milton Friedman, William Landes, Robert McCormick, Douglas North, Chris Paul, George Stigler, Robert Tollison, Gordon Tullock, and Dean Worcester. Special thanks are due to Gordon Tullock, General Editor of this series, for suggesting the book. We would also like to thank the publishers of the *Journal of Political Economy,* the *Journal of Law and Economics,* and *Public Choice* for allowing us to reprint parts of articles from those journals. Chapter 3 was written in collaboration with Donald Keenan, and the econometric appendix was written by Carter Hill, who generally helped with the econometrics. Finally, the name order of the authors of the book is alphabetical; both authors contributed equally to the effort.

INTRODUCTION

In a sense, this book might seem like a strange undertaking for two economists. The material seems to be much closer to political science than to economics; our topic is the determinants of congressional voting. Legislatures and roll call voting are traditionally in the domain of political science. This introduction is intended to explain why we have found this book worth writing.

Today the economy functions in a regulated framework. Whether or not there ever was a "golden age" of laissez faire capitalism is an issue for historians; such an age does not now exist. One implication of the high degree of politicization of the modern economy is that one cannot any longer study economics divorced from politics. The rise to prominence of the field of public choice is one strong piece of evidence about what many economists see as the significant influence of the political sector over what would seem to be purely economic variables. A more homey example may also be used to illustrate the phenomenon of increased politicization of the economy. All economists have had the experience of lecturing on the unemployment-creating effects of a minimum wage or on the shortage-creating implications of price controls, only to have a student ask: "But if that is so, why do we have those laws?" One way of viewing this book is as an attempt to answer that question.

1

It should be noted that we have a normative bias: We believe that much of the new regulation is inefficient and that the world would be a better place if it had not been passed. In one sense, it was this political belief that led us to study the causes of regulation. However, one need not share our belief in order to read this book. If one believes that such regulation as has occurred in the last ten or fifteen years is desirable, one may still ask why the regulation was not passed earlier, and the material in this book may be useful in answering that question. We do feel, however, that we should set forth our normative position for readers.

The intellectual evolution of the book is clear from the order of the chapters. We began with a certain set of goals and a certain set of research questions in mind. As we developed tools appropriate for answering those questions, it became apparent that the same tools could be used for answering other questions. First we discuss the questions with which we began; next we provide some answers to those questions; finally, we indicate other uses for the tools that we developed along the way.

The questions with which we began were questions relating to the causes of regulation in the economy. A few years ago economists had a well-developed theory of regulation: Regulation occurred when there was some market failure. Thus, the theory of regulation was a subset of welfare economics, and the goal of regulatory economists was to devise efficient tools to enable regulatory authorities to better serve the public interest. However, as economists began to study regulation, they noted a curious fact: Much, or most, regulation occurred in cases where no market failure was apparent, and the purpose of much regulation seemed to be the creation of wealth for one or another set of special interests in the economy. In fact, economists found that this pattern of regulation, which had been considered an anomaly, was the general rule; they discovered little relation between market failure and regulation. Some economists (notably George Stigler and his students) therefore proposed a different theory of regulation—namely, regulation is a good sold by legislatures and bought by special interests, and no necessary (or even likely) relationship exists between market failure and regulation. This theory, first formally proposed by Stigler in 1971, was the theory that we believed when we began our research for this book.

Stigler's theory, however, had some difficulties that were magnified over time. While it explained one set of regulations quite well, other regulations were arising, even as the theory was put forth, that did not lend themselves to the same explanation. For example, the theory explained well the regulation of transportation by the Interstate Commerce Commission when the regulation could be shown to benefit trains and trucks. But the theory did a poor job of explaining National Highway Traffic Safety Administration regulation of automobile safety, which could not be shown to benefit anyone, let alone the automobile industry. Moreover, in the 1960s and 1970s regulations of the latter type were expanding. Thus, our problem was to explain this new type of regulation within the framework proposed by Stigler; as chapter 1 makes clear, we were not successful in solving this problem.

When the economic explanation advanced by Stigler seemed unable to explain observed patterns of regulation, we turned to an alternative theory of regulation based on ideology—that is, a set of beliefs about the structure of the world and ways of improving it. Ideology was not a concept familiar to economists or a concept with which economists had dealt in detail. In order to find an economist who had written about ideology in a useful manner, we had to return to the work of Joseph Schumpeter, and in particular to *Capitalism, Socialism, and Democracy* (1950). In this book Schumpeter set forth a theory of the fall of capitalism based in part on what he perceived as the increasing hostility of intellectuals toward capitalism. Schumpeter's beliefs about the importance of ideology are strongly opposed by George Stigler, who states explicitly that economic self-interest, not ideas, is important in influencing legislation. In chapter 2 we present these two views in more detail and attempt to derive some implications from them. We find that Schumpeter's view is not completely consistent and needs some modification; nonetheless, it does provide the basis for a testable hypothesis that may be contrasted with Stigler's view.

We are concerned with laws. In the United States all national laws are passed by Congress. Thus, if we are to determine the forces behind passage of particular laws, we must determine why representatives vote for or against certain bills. Therefore, we decided that roll call voting by Congress would provide a set of data for our examination of the laws with which we were concerned. In chapter 3 we discuss roll call voting. We indicate the sorts of questions that political scientists have used these data to answer, and we indicate the problems with the models of political scientists. (Much of the work of political scientists was done some years ago; therefore, many of their problems are due to weak data bases and methods of statistical analysis. Better sources of data and better statistical techniques, which were not available earlier, have recently become available.) We identify three agents who are important in the roll call voting model: representatives, who actually vote for the bills; constituents, who vote for or against representatives based on the stands of the representatives on issues of interest to constituents; and contributors to political campaigns, who give to representatives based on the way the representatives will vote on issues of interest to the contributors. Simultaneous relationships exist between all these agents: Representatives vote in part as contributors desire, but contributors also give to representatives with certain propensities. Similar results hold for constituents. Thus, to disentangle the effects of various factors on congressional voting and to be able to answer the questions with which we started, we specified a simultaneous model of behavior of all three agents. In the last part of chapter 3 we provide the theoretical basis for such a simultaneous equations model.

In part II we perform various empirical tests of our hypotheses. The central issue in this part of the book is the extent to which ideological factors, as opposed to economic factors, explain roll call voting. We provide several tests.

Chapter 4 is an examination of the role of public interest lobbies in the passage of legislation. These lobbies are ideological in nature — that is, people join and contribute for reasons that are not totally economic. (In fact, the economic theory of political participation cannot explain the existence of public interest lobbies.) The question we ask is whether these lobbies have any impact on congressional voting. If they do, ideological factors may be significant in explaining voting. We conclude from our observations, even after controlling for economic factors, that the lobbies do have an impact: Representatives from states with many members of public interest lobbies seem to vote as the lobbies want. This result is from a single equation model, and the measure of ideology may be suspect. Nonetheless, it does provide a first bit of evidence about the role of ideology in influencing legislation.

In chapter 5 we examine congressional voting on minimum wages, an issue of some interest to economists. Estimations in this chapter are based on a single equation model, where we examine the impact of constituency on voting by representatives. We adjust for several economic variables: race, average hourly earnings in the representative's district, union membership in the state, and political party. As a measure of ideology, we use the representative's ADA rating. Again we find that the ideological variable is significant in explaining voting. Moreover, these results are for the period 1949–1974, and we find stability in the results over this time period. We thus provide a second test for the importance of ideology.

In chapter 6 we examine voting on several types of issues. Again we control for economic interests of constituents and use ADA ratings as a measure of ideology. In this chapter we also allow for the possibility that ADA ratings are a measure of membership in a voting coalition, so that what appears to be ideology may actually be a form of logrolling. We find that this hypothesis is not tenable; ideology is something more than membership in a coalition. Thus we have a further piece of evidence about the importance of ideology in explaining voting.

Chapter 7 is the most important empirical chapter in the book. In this chapter we estimate the full simultaneous equations model of congressional voting, constituent voting, and contributions to political campaigns. We find that the model provides a good fit for the data, and that many of the economic variables are important in explaining voting. Nonetheless, our measures of ideology — voting for Ford in the 1976 presidential election in the representative's district and ADA ratings — are the most significant variables in explaining voting by the representative on all bills examined. We argue that, after adjustment for the economic factors, these factors are measures of ideology, and therefore the evidence is consistent with the hypothesis that voting is ideologically determined. As a check on the robustness of our results, we estimate two systems of equations — one system dealing with voting on general issues and one system dealing with voting on urban issues. We find that the results are highly consistent between the two systems, which indicates that our specification is correct. We find that voting by representatives is significant in explaining the contributions that they receive (unions give to liberal representatives and business and medical contributors give to conservatives), and contributions from unions are significant in explaining congressional voting, but contributions from business have no impact on such voting.

Chapter 7 serves as the final test of our hypothesis of the importance of ideology. In the process of testing this hypothesis, we have developed a rather complete system of equations that explains a good deal about the behavior of Congress. Moreover, our data on campaign contributions are more complete than any previously available; therefore, the estimates based on these data are more complete than any previous estimates in the literature.

In part III we apply the evidence we have developed to two issues of some current importance. In chapter 8 we compare voting in 1978 with voting in 1972. In the period between these two years, political action committees (PACs) became more important in the political process. Thus, by comparing these years, we are able to obtain some evidence about the importance of PACs. We find that PACs have had relatively little impact on unions; in both 1972 and 1978 unions gave primarily to liberal representatives, and union contributions served to increase the liberalism of representatives. However, PACs seem to have had more impact on business contributors. In 1972 business gave to representatives independently of the voting behavior of the representatives, and business contributions did not affect congressional voting. In 1978 business gave primarily to conservative representatives, though contributions still had no impact on the voting behavior of recipients. We also discuss the law allowing formation of PACs and observe that, though passage seems to have been favored by union representatives, the law seems primarily to have benefited business.

In chapter 9 we consider the issue of the "price" of Congress. We estimate the amount of contributions required from various types of contributors to change the ideological orientation of Congress by specified amounts and find that such estimates are meaningful. The techniques that we have developed could also be used to estimate the cost of changing voting by Congress or by individual representatives on any sort of bill.

Chapter 10 summarizes our findings and indicates possible future research directions. The techniques and methods that we have developed should be useful to students of politics as well as to economists concerned with the impetus for passage of various types of laws.

The appendix deals with the econometrics used in the book, particularly in chapter 7. We assume that readers are familiar with regression analysis. We first develop an analysis of probit and logit, techniques of estimation when the dependent variable is dichotomous (e.g., a "yes" or "no" vote on a bill) and thus techniques particularly useful for estimating equations where the dependent variables are votes. Next we develop the analysis for simultaneous equations estimation with dichotomous dependent variables that is necessary when some equations are dichotomous and others (e.g., the equation explaining constituent voting and the equations explaining contributions) are not. An econometrician should be able to develop techniques for performing the sort of analysis we have performed; general readers should have a greater appreciation for the kinds of results that we have developed.

I THEORY

1 THE PROBLEM:
Economic Analysis and the Rise of New Regulation

Casual observation and empirical analysis indicate that the framework in which the economy operates is becoming increasingly politicized. More and more aspects of economic behavior have become subject to political control, and this trend seems to be accelerating. Weidenbaum (1981), for example, lists forty-two major regulatory acts passed between 1962 and 1978. Furthermore, many of the new regulations have extremely broad impacts. So-called old regulation generally applied to firms operating within particular industries. The Interstate Commerce Commission (ICC), for example, originally regulated railroads and, later, trucks; the Civil Aeronautics Board (CAB) regulated air transport; the Federal Communications Commission (FCC) regulated communications. The Securities and Exchange Commission (SEC), founded in 1934, regulated the capital-raising activities of all firms, but from the founding of the SEC until 1962, general regulation of economic activity was relatively rare. Since 1962 general regulation has greatly increased. For example, the Environmental Protection Agency (EPA), an agency of the "new" regulation, oversees certain activities of all firms, as does the Occupational Safety and Health Administration (OSHA), the Consumer Product Safety Commission (CPSC), and the Equal Employment Opportunity Commission (EEOC).

Almost no area of a typical business firm's activity is unaffected by government regulation. In economic theory a firm combines inputs (labor, capital, and land, including natural resources) in order to produce output for sale; the firm's profit is the difference between the purchase price of the inputs and the selling price of the output. Government regulation now affects each aspect of this process. The raising of capital is governed by the SEC; the use of land is regulated by the EPA; the use of energy is regulated by the Department of Energy (DOE). Labor is perhaps the most regulated input of all: Hiring and promotion standards are governed by the EEOC; wages may be affected by the Fair Labor Standards Act, which mandates, among other things, minimum wages and overtime pay rates; workplace safety standards are governed by OSHA; the employee pension plan is controlled by ERISA. The firm's output, or product, is also governed by regulation: The CPSC deals with product safety, the National Highway and Traffic Safety Administration (NHTSA) with automobile safety, and the FDA with standards for food and drugs. Advertising is regulated by the FTC, and pricing policy may be subject to antitrust ruling by the FTC or by the Justice Department.

THEORIES OF ECONOMIC REGULATION

Since the time of Adam Smith economists have been concerned with the effect of regulatory laws on the economy. Traditionally, their concern has taken two forms. Some economists, concerned with normative matters, attempted to devise optimal types of regulation to eliminate or mitigate instances of market failure. The theoretical basis for this school of analysis was welfare economics — that is, proponents assumed that government is benevolent and concerned with maximizing consumer welfare and that if economists could devise efficient rules, government would adopt these rules. Kahn's (1970) two-volume work on regulation is an example of this type of analysis.

Another school of analysis examined the effects of government regulation. Much of the resulting literature was empirical — that is, it actually measured the costs and benefits of various types of regulations (for some recent examples, see Peltzman 1973, 1975). This literature concluded that much government regulation was counterproductive. For example, economists found that minimum wage laws led to increased unemployment among people who were supposedly benefited by such laws. In other instances, Peltzman (1973) found that the 1962 amendments to the Food and Drug Act (the Kefauver amendments) probably served to increase the number of ill people who died or whose conditions worsened, since the amendments served mainly to reduce the number of drugs on the market without increasing the usefulness of drugs that were marketed. Again, Peltzman (1975) found that the 1966 Traffic Safety Act did not seem to reduce automobile-related fatalities. Most students of the early regulatory agencies had also found instances of counterproductive regulation. For example, the ICC seemed to encourage formation of cartels in the transportation industry and to benefit firms in the industry at the expense of consumers (MacAvoy 1965). Surprisingly, Stigler and Friedland (1962) found virtually no effect from state regulation of electric utilities, but more recently Jarrell (1978) found that such regulation served to raise prices and profits in states that adopted regulation early.

Thus, these two schools of analysis seemed contradictory. On the one hand, economists had devised many rules for optimal or efficient regulation; on the other hand, accumulating evidence indicated that little, if any, regulation seemed to address the problems that economists had identified. Indeed, much of the regulation seemed to be counterproductive. This situation led Coase (1960) to point out that it was not useful to compare a perfectly functioning government with the actual workings of the market, since government did not seem in general to function perfectly. Rather, Coase argued, before making policy recommendations, economists should compare the actual functioning of government with the actual functioning of markets. (Coase's paper was the inspiration for many later studies of the actual functioning of regulation.) Jordan (1972) pointed out empirically that regulation of industries did not seem to conform to the economic model, which would indicate that primarily natural monopolies would be regulated.

A third school of economic analysis offers a partial solution to the problems of economic regulation. *Public choice* is the branch of economics and political science that assumes rational self-interest as the criterion of behavior of agents in the political process. The literature in this field is based on the assumption that people in the political sector behave in much the same way that they behave in the economic sector. Thus, we cannot assume a priori that elected or appointed government officials attempt to maximize some part of the public interest; rather, public officials are just as likely to attempt to maximize their own self-interest as are agents in the business sector. To explain the behavior of government, then, we must determine how self-interest becomes filtered through the political process. Early and important works in this tradition are Downs (1957), Buchanan and Tullock (1962), and Olson (1965); a recent summary is available in Mueller (1979).

Stigler (1971) began the process of relating the economic model of self-interest-maximizing behavior to the passage of specific regulatory laws. He argued that laws are like any other goods; they are produced by legislatures and sold to interest groups, which are "buyers" of legislation. Stigler's model makes no presumption that laws will bear any relationship to the public interest, however defined; rather, laws will serve to benefit concentrated minorities. This analysis was extended by Rubin (1975), who argued that the form of the laws passed was determined not only by the demanders (the special-interest groups) but also by the political agents, who would pass laws that would allow themselves to obtain part of the rents created by the laws.

Peltzman (1976) also made an important contribution to the literature of public choice. He started with the assumption that regulators were interested in maximizing the political majority they would achieve from any given regulatory action. Any type of regulation would produce gainers and losers. Peltzman pointed out that we should not in general expect the gainers to gain everything they wanted; rather, the observed result should be a compromise. Thus, for example, a cartel of producers formed by government should be less desirable than a cartel formed without government intervention (where such a cartel is possible), since the cartel formed independently of government would more closely approximate a monopoly solution. When a monopoly is regulated prices and profits would be lower than in a pure monopoly, while when competitive firms are regulated prices and profits should rise higher than those in an unregulated market (though not as high as those on the monopoly level).

The models based on the theory of rational self-interest differ somewhat from the *capture theory of regulation* advanced by political scientists. According to this theory, regulatory agencies are set up to perform some function in the public interest and initially do so. However, after some time the initiators of the regulation lose interest, but the regulated firms do not. Thus, firms that were once regulated are ultimately able to capture the regulatory authority and pervert it for their own ends. The models we have discussed do not assume the existence of any initial phase of public service; rather, the purpose of a regulatory agency is always to benefit the regulated group, and this group, therefore, has no need to "capture" the agency. Posner (1974) has compared the capture theory with the economic theory and the public interest theory of regulation.

The Stigler-Peltzman analyses are based on the theory of rational, self-interested voting. According to this theory, individuals as voters are concerned primarily with the impact of government decisions on their personal incomes. If the gains from some law are concentrated among a relatively small group and the losses are diffused throughout the electorate, then, normally, public officials feel some incentive for passage of the bill because the bill will be a strong issue for the gainers. Members of the gaining group will decide how to vote in future elections based solely on the behavior of candidates toward the interest of the group. For example, farmers might be expected to vote for or against representatives solely on the basis of the representatives' stand on farm issues. Downs (1957) demonstrated that candidates can be elected by taking a minority interest on all issues; Buchanan and Tullock (1962) made essentially the same point in their discussion of logrolling. The theory of rational self-interest, though expressed in terms of the voting decisions of interest groups, also applies to activities such as political contributions. For example, contributors from the oil industry would have a strong interest in candidates' voting records on bills affecting this industry and would concentrate their contributions accordingly.

Stigler (1971) took the theory of rational, self-interested voting and applied it to regulatory decisions; he argued that we should generally expect regulations to benefit the regulated because the regulated have a strong interest in the form of the regulation. Likewise, Peltzman (1976) showed that politicians' interest in maximizing their majority would dictate that the minority interest would not get all it wanted; other minorities would also be represented in the final decision.

The theory of regulation based on rational self-interest is able to explain much regulatory legislation of the past. That the ICC served primarily to benefit railroads initially and trucks later, or that the CAB serves primarily to benefit airlines, is not surprising in light of this theory; the railroad and airline industries would have strong interests in the functioning of the ICC and the CAB, respectively, and would lobby and have their members vote in accordance with those interests. Rather than arguing that the regulatory agencies have been "captured" by the industries they were set up to regulate, Stigler (1971) argues that the agencies were actually set up to form cartels within the industries and are, therefore, serving their function when cartels appear. Stigler, in fact, argues that it is no more appropriate to criticize the ICC for benefiting the transportation industry than to criticize the Great Atlantic and Pacific Tea Company for selling groceries; each organization should be expected to perform the function for which it was designed. The theory of self-interested behavior has recently been extended by McCormick and Tollison (1981).

ECONOMIC ANALYSIS AND THE NEW REGULATION

While analysis based on self-interested behavior can explain much of the old-style regulation, it has a good deal more difficulty in explaining many recent regulations. In some cases the beneficiaries of the newer regulation are not interest groups but consumer groups. Thus, the main beneficiaries of environmental legislation are consumers with an interest in cleaner air, in wilderness hiking, and in other environmental aspects affected by the legislation. Contrary to what the theory of self-interest might predict, consumer groups do seem to have effectively organized in recent years to influence legislation. For example, the National Rifle Association, primarily a consumer group, wields considerable political power. Though consumer group influence is somewhat surprising, however, it is not completely inconsistent with the self-interest theory, since consumers may have strong interest in something they consume; thus, they may be motivated to influence legislation.

More puzzling is the passage of various laws that relate primarily to safety. One early example is the 1962 amendments to the Food and Drug Act (the Kefauver amendments); more recent examples include automobile safety laws, consumer product safety laws, and occupational safety laws. The existence of these laws is surprising because, so far as analysis can determine, no one has benefited from their passage. As justification for such a strong statement, let us examine some laws that regulate safety and then discuss the empirical evidence that forms the basis of our statement.

Consider automobile safety, which has been regulated since 1966. An important analytical distinction (though one that has not been made by law) exists between rules that affect the occupants of cars and rules that affect others. Laws mandating seat belts, for example, affect only passengers in automobiles; laws regulating brakes and lights affect third parties, such as pedestrians and other drivers. Let us examine safety regulations that benefit drivers and passengers in terms of the operation of a market in which people can themselves choose how much safety to purchase. Seat belts were available as options before they were mandated by law. Some cars have always been safer than others; for example, the Mercedes, for those who want to spend more on safety, has always been available. Ford, too, in 1958 offered relatively safe cars equipped with features such as padded dashboards; they found, however, that consumers were not willing to pay for additional safety. In short, anyone who wanted a safer-than-average car has always been able to purchase one. The history of automobile manufacturing shows (even before any safety regulation existed) that cars became safer as manufacturers responded to the wishes of consumers. Thus, if a law is passed that mandates more safety than consumers are willing to pay for (e.g., current proposals for air bags in automobiles), the basis for the law must be paternalistic — that is, derived from the notion that "society" or government is a better judge of individual welfare than are individuals themselves. Even given the fact of a paternalistic government, regulations remain puzzling. For example, evidence indicates that safety laws have not, in fact, reduced auto-related fatalities (see Peltzman 1975); thus, we have a law that imposes substantial costs and has no measurable benefits. Another puzzle is why, when laws are passed by a democratic process, voters (who are also consumers of automobiles), should vote to require safety devices that they, as consumers, choose not to purchase.

Analysis of safety equipment that affects others besides passengers in cars leads to a different conclusion. For example, consider braking systems; cars are now required to have dual braking systems, so that if the fluid leaks out of one brake cylinder, two of the brakes will still have fluid and the car will be able to stop. If cars did not have such systems, perhaps more accidents would occur. Assume, however, that the market offers cars with and without such systems. Purchasers would then decide whether or not to buy additional safety. They would consider the marginal cost of the braking system, which they must pay, as well as the marginal benefit (the reduced probability of being harmed in an accident). Other people also benefit from an individual's purchase of a dual braking system because an individual with such a system is less likely to harm others in an accident — that is, the possession of a dual braking system creates external benefits. However, a consumer might well ignore external benefits when deciding whether or not to purchase dual brakes, since the consumer has no property rights over the savings to others that the purchase may create. In the case of some safety devices, then, an argument can be made that the market will underprovide them; therefore, a theoretical case exists for government support of such devices, either in the form of mandated safety standards (the form of support now used) or of government subsidies to purchasers of cars equipped with certain safety devices. However, this argument applies only to safety devices that create external benefits; the argument for devices whose benefits are only internalized (e.g., seat belts or air bags) can have no basis but paternalism.

However, the various laws that have mandated safety devices have not made any distinction between external and internal benefits; the laws have regulated brake systems, but they have also mandated seat belts, shoulder harnesses, and collapsible steering columns. Currently, the NHTSA is also considering the mandating of air bags, devices that create no external benefit but only serve during crashes to protect occupants of automobiles who have chosen not to use seat belts. Thus, though a theoretical case can be made for certain types of safety equipment, the fact that the laws have indiscriminately mandated equipment with and without external effects is an indication that the motives of the advocates of increased safety legislation are paternalistic. Agencies charged with regulating automobile safety seem to have been substituting their judgment for the judgment of consumers. Presumably, paternalistic motives were also the basis for the congressional decision to set up the safety agency.

The argument in favor of mandated safety devices that create external benefits is somewhat weakened when we consider the function of liability rules in accident cases. Posner (1977) views the tort system as an attempt to force people to internalize the external costs of their actions. Thus, if a person has an accident because his brakes fail, and if it can be shown that his negligence contributed to the brake failure, he will be held liable. However, the tort system is weakened by two factors. First, the existence of insurance weakens the link between the amount of safety purchased by drivers and the costs they must bear, since liability will be covered by insurance (the well-known moral hazard problem). Second, the courts generally do not mandate radically new technology. For example, if a car causing an accident had single brakes that were not adequately maintained, the driver might be found negligent and liable. However, it is highly unlikely that courts would find a driver negligent for not having a dual braking system if no other car on the road had such a system. Thus, though the liability system weakens the argument for mandating some safety devices, it is still likely that market failure would be present in regard to some safety equipment.

What is the result of a cost-benefit calculation of laws relating to automobile safety? This question was addressed by Peltzman (1975). Analysis by safety engineers of the effects of safety equipment usually begins with an examination of actual crashes to determine how the occupants fared with certain safety equipment relative to how they would have fared without the equipment. The conclusion generally reached from this sort of analysis is that occupants are greatly benefited by the equipment in question. However, Peltzman realized that this sort of analysis is seriously incomplete because if a consumer is forced to buy a safer car than he would prefer, he might be expected to compensate by increasing the riskiness of driving, perhaps by driving faster or more carelessly. Moreover, even before the passage of automobile safety laws in 1966, cars had been becoming safer in response to consumer demands, so that it is incorrect to view the decrease in fatalities that occurred after 1966 as entirely a result of these laws. Peltzman attempted to control for these factors in a time series study of automobile fatalities; he concluded that the laws had absolutely no effect on the number of automobile-related fatalities. Drivers and passengers in cars were, in fact, made safer by the laws, but pedestrians were actually made less safe; the decrease in fatalities of drivers exactly compensated for the increase in pedestrian fatalities — the result one might expect if drivers were compensating for safer cars by driving more recklessly.

We thus have a puzzle when we attempt to explain laws mandating safer cars. Even if the laws worked as designed, little theoretical basis exists for them since many of the reforms they mandate create no external benefits. Furthermore, we are unable to identify any interest group that could be expected to benefit from these laws; automobile manufacturers, for example, seem to have been major losers. In sum, automobile safety laws do not seem to serve any purpose at all, and yet they have imposed substantial costs on the economy.

Safety regulation in other areas creates many similar puzzles. For example, in 1962, in response to the thalidomide controversy, Congress passed a law strengthening the power of the FDA to regulate drugs. (Procedures in effect before 1962 were already adequate to keep thalidomide off of the U.S. market; thus, the problems caused by this drug seem to constitute a weak argument for strengthening drug regulation.) Requiring greater safety of new drugs exacts a price; as we require more extensive and expensive testing of drugs, some harmful drugs may be stopped, but some useful drugs will also not be marketed. Peltzman (1973), in his study of the impact of the 1962 drug amendments, concluded that drugs marketed after passage of the amendments were no more effective than drugs sold earlier. Furthermore, Wardell and Lasagna (1975) have found that the drug legislation has reduced the availability of beneficial new drugs to consumers. Again, no one seems to have benefited from this legislation (for example, Peltzman found that the laws did not lead to increases in profits for drug companies); rather, it seems to have imposed costs on consumers with no corresponding detectable benefits either to consumers or to producers.

Regulations with no obvious beneficiaries are not confined solely to laws dealing with safety. Stigler (1964), for example, found that the Securities and Exchange Commission, in its regulation of the amount of information sellers of stock were obligated to provide to buyers, had no detectable impact on the relative rate of return for investors in new issues, the most heavily regulated stocks. Benston (1977) examined many other aspects of SEC information regulation and found that, in general, disclosure laws did not benefit investors. Schwert (1977) found that the imposition of regulatory laws did not benefit securities dealers; rather, as a result of regulation the value of a seat on the New York Stock Exchange fell by about 50 percent, and this value has never been made up. Moreover, the existence of SEC regulations imposes substantial costs on business firms that desire to raise capital; costs may be especially high for relatively new or small firms. Again, then, we find a set of laws that have no detectable beneficiaries and that impose substantial costs on society.

Other forms of regulation exist that seem to benefit some special-interest groups and yet still create puzzles. An example is minimum wage laws. Economists are generally convinced that such laws serve primarily to reduce employment among low-skill workers; black teenagers are the primary, though not the only, victims (see Linneman 1980). We can, however, identify some groups that benefit from minimum wage laws. Union workers, for example, are important beneficiaries, even though union workers earn more than the minimum wage. High-wage workers benefit from the raising of the wages of low-wage workers since high-wage and low-wage workers are substitutes for each other in production; anything that raises the costs to employers of hiring low-wage workers increases the demand for high-wage workers and hence increases their incomes. Minimum wage laws also affect geographic wage differences: If southern workers earn less than north-eastern workers, increasing the wages of southern workers also serves to in-crease demand for northeastern workers. Thus, unions and northeastern workers support minimum wages, but many people who sincerely desire to help the poor also favor such laws. Perhaps through ignorance such people have convinced themselves that minimum wage laws are desirable; many people simply do not understand the workings of markets well enough to understand the effects of minimum wage laws. Many economists who have written about the ill effects of minimum wage laws believe that if the ig-norance could be dispelled, the laws might be repealed (see, for example, Friedman 1962). The extent to which the factors of ignorance and self-interest are involved in the passage of minimum wage laws is an interesting empirical question; the fact that laws have been passed with no detectable benefits for anyone indicates that we cannot a priori rule out ignorance as a potential explanation.

Other instances of questionable regulation abound. OSHA, for example, does not seem to have had any effect on industrial safety (Viscusi 1979). Posner (1977) offers an explanation for the creation of OSHA: The regula-tions it mandates might serve to increase costs for unsafe firms, which generally employ low-wage (and hence non-union) labor. Thus, OSHA regulations would also increase demand for union labor, just as minimum wage laws serve to increase demand for union workers. However, this argu-ment seems to imply that employers who have relatively safe workplaces would prefer even more safety regulation (since costs for competitors would therefore be increased), and no evidence of this preference exists. Also, while some OSHA regulations may benefit workers, many other regulations do not. Finally, the regulatory mechanism seems to be an extremely roundabout way to increase demand for union workers as well as an extremely uncertain one; it is impossible to predict how a new and powerful government agency will act. Thus, Posner's argument is not convincing in the absence of em-pirical testing. OSHA seems, rather, to be part of a recent increase in regulatory agencies of all sorts — agencies that, as we have seen, promulgate many laws whose benefits are not readily apparent.

Some scholars argue that government regulators, viewed as an interest group, benefit from increased regulation — in principle, a potentially convincing argument. Niskanen (1971), for example, has shown that bureaucrats have an interest in maintaining the power of their own bureaus. However, many of the regulations discussed in this chapter have involved the setting up of new bureaus. While a few bureaucrats might have known that they would go to work for ERISA once ERISA began to function, one would not expect this kind of prescience to be common. Bureaucrats may have a general interest in increasing demands for their services by increasing the size of government, but such general interest would be a rather weak incentive for creating particular agencies. Thus, the benefits that increased regulation confer on bureaucrats do not appear, without empirical testing, to be a strong enough argument to explain the new regulations.

Even if we were able to identify agents who benefit from the recent increase in regulatory laws, we would not have a complete explanation for the passage of these laws; a full explanation must include not only the beneficiaries, but also the timing of the laws. We must show why the groups that benefit from the laws have only recently been able to obtain sufficient political power to pass these laws. This requirement must be met no matter what our theory of legislation is. If we believe, for example, that the purpose and effect of regulatory laws is really to improve safety, we still must ask why the problem of unsafe products or unsafe working conditions has suddenly become so severe that regulation is needed now but was not needed in the past. One possibility is that rising income has led to an increased demand for safety. That is, we may argue that safety is a normal or superior good, in that demand for safety increases with increases in income. Since the incomes of Americans have increased over time, increased demands for safety might logically follow, and some of this increased demand would be satisfied by legally mandating safety regulations. However, there is no obvious reason why we should rely on government to achieve the desired increase in safety. In the case of transactions between parties (as opposed to third-party effects), we would expect increased demand for safety to lead firms to provide increased safety. Indeed, the evidence is consistent with this expectation: Chelius (1977) has demonstrated that as incomes of workers have increased, workplace safety has also increased. Similarly, Peltzman (1975) has shown that, even before the existence of the NHTSA, automobile safety had increased. The market seems to have responded on its own to increased demand for safety caused by increased incomes; increased demand, then, should not have led to increased regulation. Thus, no matter what theory we may have for the increase in safety regulation, an explanation for its timing as well as for its existence is still needed.

*   *   *

In sum, a reasonably well-developed economic theory of legislation holds that, in general, laws are passed for the benefit of relatively concentrated special interests. This theory can explain much of the older regulatory legislation, such as the benefits conferred on the broadcasting industry by the FCC. However, the theory has some trouble explaining much of the newer legislation, which often deals with matters of safety and health (though other areas, such as pension funds, are also regulated). While it is sometimes possible to identify interest groups that might benefit from the new laws, the beneficiaries are not always apparent. In short, much of the new legislation seems to impose substantial costs on the economy and to benefit no one. The research contained in the following chapters is aimed at determining the causes of the new regulatory legislation. To do so we must examine in some detail the workings of the political sector because this sector seems to have a large and growing impact on the functioning of the economy.

2 IDEOLOGY:
An Explanation for Public Policy Making

A possible explanation for the passage of the laws discussed in chapter 1 would be ideology. We will not develop an elaborate definition of ideology here; Downs's definition, "a verbal image of the good society and of the chief means of constructing such a society" (1957, p. 96), is sufficient. For purposes of analysis we may identify two ideological positions that political agents (voters, politicians, bureaucrats, and contributors) may take: A pro-market position argues for reducing the scope of government regulation of economic activity below current levels; an antimarket position favors more government intervention and generally opposes the use of markets.

As we saw in chapter 1, many laws seem to have no effect on the economy or to have harmful effects. We may identify three potential explanations for the passage of such laws. One possibility is simple error: Legislators have passed laws to accomplish certain goals, such as reduction of automobile-related fatalities or creation of safer workplaces, and the laws have simply been ineffective. As Moore says: "Law is based on folk notions of social causality" (1978, p. 7), so that it is not impossible that laws are passed because of error. However, problems arise when we use error as an explanation for useless or harmful regulation. First, the hypothesis is not falsifiable because any observed behavior is consistent with an argument that says that an error occurred. Thus, unless we have some theory of error, an explanation based on mistake is tautological and hence not useful for scientific purposes. Second, while we may want to allow error as an explanation for a single occurrence of some phenomenon, its use as explanation for a whole series of laws seems to be pushing the concept too far. Agents probably would not make the same, possibly expensive, error repeatedly. At any rate, we would not want to use error as an explanation unless we had exhausted all other possible hypotheses.

Stigler (1971) presents a second explanation for useless or harmful regulation. He argues that all laws are passed to benefit some particular interest; when we are unable to explain the passage of some laws, we simply have not looked hard enough. This position, though consistent, appears untenable on the evidence discussed in chapter 1. Laws that we thought we understood (e.g., the Securities and Exchange Act) are inexplicable within the self-interest framework (Schwert 1977), and other inexplicable laws (e.g., the various safety laws) are continually being passed. Posner (1974) argued that the economic theory of regulation had not been applied to the "consumerist" laws; his statement is still true, and yet today there are more such laws. Thus, while we might want to keep looking for interest groups that benefit from these laws, we might also assume, at least provisionally, that other explanations for these laws are possible.

The third possible explanation for superfluous legislation — an explanation that is not inconsistent with the empirical evidence available — is that part of the motivation of legislative agents is ideological. Most economists (and indeed, most intellectuals) believe that ideas play an important role in the passage of legislation. Economists are fond of quoting Keynes's statement:

> The ideas of economists and political philosophers, both when they are right and when they are wrong, are more powerful than is commonly understood. Indeed, the world is ruled by little else. Practical men, who believe themselves to be quite exempt from any intellectual influences, are usually the slaves of some defunct economist. Madmen in authority, who hear voices in the air, are distilling their frenzy from some academic scribbler of a few years back. I am sure that the power of vested interests is vastly exaggerated compared with the gradual encroachment of ideas. Not, indeed, immediately, but after a certain interval; for in the field of economic and political philosophy there are not many who are influenced by new theories after they are 25 or 30 years of age, so that the ideas which civil servants and politicians and even agitators apply to current events are not of the newest. But, soon or late, it is ideas, not vested interests, which are dangerous for good or evil. [Keynes 1936, p. 383]

Whenever economists end articles with policy statements, they are implicitly arguing for the importance of ideas in influencing legislation, and this view is shared by virtually all social scientists. To take an example almost at random, we find Nisbet arguing: "We live, it has often been said, under the spell of ideas, good or bad, true or false. We may think we are responding directly to events and changes in the histories of institutions, but we aren't; we are responding to these events and changes as they are made real or assimilable to us by ideas already in our heads" (1980, p. 4).

The fact that intellectuals — people who make their living presenting and arguing about ideas — think that ideas are influential does not prove them so. Indeed, it would be surprising if intellectuals generally took any other position; we do not normally expect the sellers of a product to denigrate its importance. So the virtually unanimous agreement by intellectuals (save Stigler) on the importance of ideas is not itself persuasive evidence for the correctness of this position (nor is it evidence against its correctness; some products for which sellers claim importance are, in fact, important). The issue must be examined independently of the claims of those who sell ideas.

Though economists generally seem to believe that ideas are influential, they have not devoted much formal effort to developing theories of the influence of ideas on legislation. Schumpeter and Stigler, two scholars who have done so, hold opposing positions: Schumpeter feels that ideas are very important in any explanation of political action; Stigler feels that they are not. Let us examine each position in greater detail.

SCHUMPETER'S THEORY

Schumpeter (1950) predicts the fall of capitalism through several mechanisms, one of which is the growing power of "intellectuals." Capitalism creates increasing wealth that, in turn, creates a class of people who depend on ideas for their livelihood. Intellectuals have always existed in society, but as incomes increase, the number of intellectuals also increases because greater wealth leads to more widespread literacy and thus to more demand for writers; in addition, wealthy societies provide more education, and many intellectuals are themselves educators. Thus, capitalism creates an ever larger class of intellectuals whose influence increases because more widespread literacy means that their writings will be read by more people. Schumpeter, in the 1942 edition of his work, mentioned the radio as another means of spreading the power of intellectuals; television would merely serve to further increase their influence. Moreover, the power centers in a capitalist system find it difficult, if not impossible, to suppress intellectual discourse because the essence of capitalism is reliance on rationality;

therefore, suppression of intellectuals and their ideas would be a contradiction. Thus, capitalism is unable to control the large and powerful class of intellectuals it has created.

Schumpeter also maintains that this large and powerful group of intellectuals is hostile toward the capitalist system. The reasons for their hostility are ultimately economic. First, greater returns accrue to intellectuals from criticism rather than from defense of the existing order. (Intellectuals are generally opposed to being called apologists.) Second, many intellectuals are unable to earn large incomes from employment in capitalist enterprises — a fact that becomes more salient as the number of intellectuals increases. These unemployable intellectuals are thus among the first to criticize a system that does not generate large incomes for them. Finally, intellectuals generally benefit from an expansion of government power because bureaucrats are often chosen from among intellectuals, who might otherwise be unable to obtain jobs in the private sector. Also, the public sector pays relatively more for intellectual skills than does the private sector. Thus, the incomes of intellectuals increase if the size of the public sector increases. For all these reasons, intellectuals are generally biased against capitalism and in favor of more intervention and regulation in the economy.

In addition to the power and anticapitalist bias of the intellectuals, Schumpeter (p. 153) claims that a "general hostile atmosphere . . . surrounds the capitalist engine" and that the "role of the intellectual group consists primarily in stimulating, energizing, verbalizing, and organizing this material and only secondarily in adding to it." Taking labor unions as an example, Schumpeter argues that intellectuals serve to express the ideas of workers and unions but also to exaggerate these ideas and to radicalize the unions. "Thus, though intellectuals have not created the labor movement, they have yet worked it up into something that differs substantially from what it would be without them" (p. 154). Intellectuals also serve in political party offices (not as elected representatives, but as employees) and thus influence the positions taken by political parties.[1]

STIGLER'S THEORY

In contrast to Schumpeter, Stigler believes that ideas have virtually no influence on policy. He does seem to agree on the causes of intellectuals' hostility toward capitalism. He argues that, since many intellectuals are employed by government, they can do better in the short run (i.e., a generation or two) by espousing programs that call for increasing government intervention. The main distinction between the argument of Stigler and that of

Schumpeter is that the former does not believe that intellectuals have any influence on any other group; while Schumpeter believes that intellectuals can
influence others, such as labor union members, to oppose capitalism,
Stigler, who more or less agrees that intellectuals are hostile toward
capitalism, does not believe that they can influence anyone else. Thus, intellectuals themselves might vote for, or otherwise encourage, more government intervention, but they will have no more impact than any other interest
group.

In order to test the arguments of Schumpeter and Stigler, we must first
discuss two issues: (1) the distinction between the class interests of intellectuals and the individual interests of each intellectual and (2) the role of information in the political process.

THE THEORY OF CLASS INTEREST

Schumpeter's entire analysis of the policies advocated by intellectuals is in
terms of the class interests of intellectuals. Stigler (1980, p. 13) analyzes both
class interests and individual interests, arguing first that "the self-interest of
the intellectuals is in the expansion of the government economy," and
second that "intellectuals distribute themselves among occupations and
among artistic, ethical, cultural, and political positions in such numbers as
to maximize their incomes, where incomes include amenities such as apparent influence."

The distinction between the class interests and the individual interests of
intellectuals may be illustrated by using economists as an example. Probably
no professional academic group has benefited more from the growth and expansion of government than have economists. The government employs
thousands of economists, and thousands more are employed by industry as a
direct result of the growth of government. In addition, more economists are
employed in teaching students areas of knowledge that are valuable only
because of the growth of government. Hayek (1945) points out that in a well-
functioning market economy one of the great advantages is that no one need
know much about the workings of the economy, but when the market is
replaced with regulation, it becomes necessary to understand the functioning
of the entire process. Bruce-Briggs (1979, p. 221) calculates from census
figures that in 1970, 67,000 economists were employed in the United States,
as compared with 44,000 "other social scientists." A large number of these
economists are directly employed by the government; thus, economists have
clearly benefited much more than political scientists or sociologists from the
increased size and influence of government. However, economists as a group

are generally more hostile to governmental growth. Journals that subscribe to the theories of the Chicago school of economics (e.g., the *Journal of Political Economy* and the *Journal of Law and Economics,* both edited at the University of Chicago), as well as journals that are not part of this school (e.g., the *Bell Journal of Economics,* currently edited at the University of Pennsylvania and originally edited at MIT), are replete with promarket, antiregulation articles.

Thus, if we believe in the class interest theory, the case of economists appears anomalous. However, economists would generally not subscribe to any class interest theory; rather, their analyses would be in terms of individual interests. In these terms intellectuals have no reason to advocate more government intervention, even if such intervention would increase the power and prestige of intellectuals as a group because, as Stigler (1980) has argued, individual career advancement is generally furthered by advocacy of positions opposed to the conventional wisdom, whatever that may be at any given time. Thus, those sociologists and political scientists who now advocate less government intervention (the so-called neo-conservatives) are relatively successful professionals; Friedrich Hayek and Milton Friedman, for example, two early and consistent advocates of the free market, have both won Nobel Prizes in economic science (though their awards were not based on their advocacy positions). Moreover, as government activity becomes more entrenched in the economy, an increasingly higher payoff should result from advocating less government intervention. The same argument applies as the theoretical belief in the efficacy of government increases among social scientists; in these circumstances intellectuals can be expected to attack both entrenched theoretical opinions and entrenched institutions. (Conversely, as the promarket, anti-interventionist position becomes more entrenched in the discipline of economics, a relatively higher payoff will accrue to economists who can make a convincing intellectual case for increased intervention in an area where it is now considered counterproductive.)

In other words, free riding exists in terms of advocating policies just as in other areas. If an economist argues successfully that some government regulatory program should be abolished, economists as a group may be net losers since the abolition may reduce demand for their services. Nonetheless, the particular economist who abolished the program might gain enough to compensate for sharing in the loss to the profession. Alfred Kahn, for example, may have been instrumental in abolishing the Civil Aeronautics Board and thus in reducing the demand for regulatory economists, but he went on to a more important and powerful position in government as chairman of the Council on Wage and Price Stability. If, like Stigler, we believe that the advocacy of positions has no impact on policy, since all policies are adopted in response to a corresponding set of economic self-interests, the positions advocated by intellectuals should be purely random with respect to intervention or nonintervention. Advocacy's only return would be in terms of the professional reputation gained or lost by clever presentation of one's position. But even if we disagree with Stigler, it is still not clear why intellectuals should advocate more intervention, even if this position maximizes the income of their group.

We should note that Stigler does not claim that intellectuals actually modify their positions in response to market forces — that is, his claim is not that, for example, an antiregulation economist will change position in response to the offer of a government grant. Rather, Stigler argues that economists have, at any time, a large set of views about a large set of problems, and they (and other intellectuals) will cultivate the particular views for which a market exists. Thus, though the responsiveness of intellectuals to incentives does not imply any intellectual dishonesty, the responsiveness is nonetheless real.

THE ROLE OF INFORMATION IN POLICY MAKING

The next issue that must be addressed is the role of information in influencing policy. Stigler argues that we may view policies as aimed at those goals that they do, in fact, achieve. Agents must, then, have enough information to obtain the passage of legislation that benefits them — that is, if laws accomplish what they are aimed at accomplishing, the agents responsible for the passage of the laws must have had enough information to understand the effects of the laws. In such cases there is no need for economists to attempt to influence legislation by analyzing the effects of laws because the agents responsible for passage understood in the first place what the laws would do. (Economists may still analyze the implications of laws, but for scientific reasons only; the agents responsible for passage already know what the economists will find.) For example, when economists announce that minimum wage laws cause unemployment among the poor, they are stating an irrelevant fact because no one responsible for the law really cares about the poor anyway.

If we take this view, we must ask why society chooses to spend its resources on economists and other social scientists whose studies will be disregarded. Stigler (1976) answers that society does not spend much on research economists; moreover, society does have an interest in the correct elucidation of relations between actions and events. Thus, when economists can point out new relationships, these relationships will be considered in policy making. Finally, he maintains that a "function of the economist is to propose and defend the economic policies which favor large or small groups in the economy" (p. 350).

In Stigler's view, then, economists have two functions: to discover new relationships and to propose and defend policies. To the extent that new, previously unknown, relationships exist, economists can, in fact, have some input into the social decision-making process. If new relationships are sometimes discovered, policies passed before the discovery must have been based on error. If this is so, the groups who passed the policies must not have been serving their own self-interest. But if an economist writes a paper demonstrating conclusively that "if X, then Y," how are we to know whether the relationship thus demonstrated is irrelevant? For example, economists have repeatedly shown that the minimum wage law causes unemployment. Stigler claims that, because the relationship between minimum wages and unemployment has been conclusively demonstrated and because the policy continues, economists have no impact on the legislation. However, though we may know ex post facto that the relationship was irrelevant, how could we have known it earlier? That is, when the first economist wrote the first paper demonstrating the effects of minimum wages on employment (perhaps Stigler himself), how could anyone have known that this information was irrelevant? Moreover, how do we know that minimum wages would not now be higher but for the work of economists in demonstrating their adverse effects? The latter proposition is not verifiable, but neither is the claim that the existence of laws mandating minimum wages demonstrates the ineffectiveness of economists as policy advisers. We must examine behavior both at the margin and in total.

The function of economists in defending economic policies raises more serious issues. As Posner (1974) points out, the economic theory of regulation does not explain why special-interest laws are couched, as they are, in general-interest terms. If Stigler's theory were correct — that is, if only the power of special-interest groups mattered — rhetoric to disguise the actual function of laws would be unnecessary. Advocates of minimum wage laws would simply vote their laws into effect; if asked the purpose, they would reply, "We know that this law will harm the poor by increasing unemployment among them. But it will help union members by increasing demand for high-wage workers, and we represent union workers." In fact, however, proponents of minimum wage laws talk of poverty and exploitation and justify the laws as helpful to the poor.

Stigler implicitly allows for this behavior in his discussion of ignorance and the cost of knowledge. He argues that the losers from passage of a law lose so little that it does not pay for them to become informed of the law's cost to themselves; rather, they may simply believe the propaganda put forth by the gainers. Downs (1957) calls this attitude "rational ignorance" and hypothesizes that it pays to be ignorant of many political facts; the costs of becoming informed outweigh the gains because of the trivial amount of influence any individual has on the political process. But to the extent that rational ignorance exists in the political process, there is room for information and ideas to have some impact. Economists' constant reiteration of certain ideas may provide information to voters about the impacts of certain laws. A television series such as "Free to Choose" and the book related to the series (Friedman and Friedman 1980) may reduce the cost to many voters of becoming informed and thus may make more difficult the passage of certain special-interest laws. To the extent that voters are made more aware, economists do indeed have an impact on legislation and policy.

Economists normally analyze the behavior of individuals in markets for private goods and generally assume that individuals have optimal amounts of information and make decisions accordingly. For example, most economists would not think that they, as economists, have any role in advising consumers about the correct automobile to purchase. Since individuals reap the gains and bear the costs of their private actions, economists naturally assume that people have the correct amount of information for private decision making. Similarly, few economists would accept the view that firms commonly make errors in their decisions; a more fruitful approach is to assume that firms are, in fact, maximizing profits and then to discover why apparently nonmaximizing behavior exists. Stigler seems to be carrying this view over to the political sector when he argues that economists have little role to play in providing information to political agents. However, the analogy does not necessarily succeed. Rather, information developed by economists and other social scientists that may influence policy has an important place in the political sector. Individuals should acquire an optimal amount of information before voting, just as they acquire an optimal amount of information before purchasing consumer goods. However, the optimal amount of information required for voting is very small; in fact, students of public choice are unable to explain why individuals vote at all. The act of voting, viewed as an attempt to influence policy, is irrational, since the probability of any one vote actually influencing the outcome of an election is small; moreover, voting does have definite costs. Given that one has decided to vote, then, the amount of information it pays one to acquire to determine the optimal way in which to vote is trivial. If a special-interest group argues that we need a tariff on American textiles in order to preserve the domestic textile industry for national defense purposes, a voter might well believe this argument since it would not pay to invest much effort in determining whether or not it was true. If the voter believes the argument, it would not pay, again, to invest effort in determining the cost of the tariff to an individual. In such a situation statements by social scientists about the true effects of a policy may well have an impact on decision making.

Thus, even if we accept Stigler's theory of legislation, we can allow room for ideas to influence policy. Stigler's argument that economists' conclusions do not, in fact, matter is no more than an assertion based on a weighing of magnitudes that have not been empirically measured. Whether or not his judgments about the weight of the relevant variables is correct is an empirical matter, one we discuss in part II.

In sum, ideology appears to play some role in the formation of public policy. Most social scientists believe that ideas influence policy — a belief that may be self-serving since social scientists make their living by proposing ideas. Schumpeter has presented a reasonably coherent theory of the behavior of intellectuals by arguing that intellectuals have an interest in attacking capitalism and should be successful in their attack. Stigler, on the contrary, while partly agreeing with Schumpeter, does not think intellectuals have any influence. We have found flaws in both theories: Schumpeter seems correct in saying that intellectuals as a group have an interest in attacking capitalism, but any one intellectual would also have an interest in maximizing personal income, and incomes would not necessarily be increased by an attack on capitalism. (Economists, who have benefited most among academics from the growth of government, are also professionally most hostile to this growth.) We have also found that Stigler's argument about the ineffectiveness of intellectuals and ideas in influencing policy is based on an assertion about the magnitudes of variables; his assertion must be more carefully tested than has been done heretofore. Most of his claims are about totals; he uses the existence of minimum wages or of tariffs as evidence of the ineffectiveness of economists in influencing policy. However, we also need information about marginals; we need to know if the size of minimum wages or of tariffs has been influenced by the advocacy of economists.

NOTES

1. While economists have largely neglected Schumpeter's theory of ideology, it has been adopted by a group of political scientists and sociologists commonly called *neoconservatives*. For a discussion by members of this group of the role of intellectuals in weakening the capitalist system, see Bruce-Briggs (1979). His title, *The New Class?*, seems to be a contemporary equivalent of Schumpeter's "intellectuals."

3 ROLL CALL VOTING BY CONGRESS

Discounting the possibility of simple error, we are left with two hypotheses that can explain the passage of various laws: Laws are passed to benefit various special-interest groups, or laws are passed because of ideological reasons. These hypotheses are not inconsistent: Special-interest groups may benefit from some laws, while other people may favor these laws for ideological reasons, although the strong form of the special-interest argument advanced by Stigler (1971) would be inconsistent with any argument based on ideology. In order to discriminate between these hypotheses, we now need to examine data; theoretical argument can take us no further.

A natural source of data about the passage of laws is data on roll call voting by Congress — data that has been used extensively by political scientists. Each roll call vote supplies up to 435 available observations; since members of Congress differ in terms of who their constituents are and of other influences on their voting, roll call data provide a natural source of information on factors that influence the passage of legislation.

DISTINCTIONS BETWEEN POLITICAL SCIENCE AND ECONOMIC ANALYSES

The fundamental problems addressed by political scientists in their use of roll call data are different from the problems with which we are concerned.

31

Political scientists are basically concerned with the methods of decision making in Congress; we are concerned with this issue only insofar as it is necessary to model the decision-making process in order to determine which groups support which laws. As we have extended our research, we have derived an essentially complete model of the congressional decision-making process, but we have always viewed this model as a tool for measuring influences on particular pieces of legislation rather than as a goal in itself. (The theoretical model is explicated in this chapter and the empirical results of the complete model are presented in chapter 7.)

The difference between our goals and those of political scientists has had important implications for the types of questions we have asked relative to the questions asked by political scientists. (The major political scientists we examined were Fiorina 1974, Matthews and Stimson 1975, Jackson 1974, Kingdon 1973, and Schneider 1979). Fiorina has an excellent summary of the pre-1974 literature, so we did not personally examine this literature. Since the mid-1970s political scientists seem to have been much less interested in roll call voting analysis. (A summary is available in Weisberg 1978.) One question that has preoccupied political scientists is the extent to which representatives vote on the basis of the interests of their constituencies and the extent to which they vote to represent their own interests. Although this question is important in democratic theory, and although our empirical results do have something to say about this issue, it is not an issue we have addressed directly. Rather, we assumed from the beginning of our research that members of Congress represented their constituents and that by determining who the constituents of a given member were and how that member voted, we would be able to determine which constituent groups desired which type of legislation. (Indeed, not until our research was substantially complete did we realize that some doubt existed about whether or not members of Congress actually did represent constituents.) Our results, discussed in part II, indicate that our strategy was not incorrect: Constituent interests do seem important in the passage of legislation. Where certain constituents have strong reason to favor some bill, we generally find that members of Congress from districts with significant numbers of these constituents do, in fact, vote for the bill in question.

Another distinction between our work and much of the work of political scientists is that the latter are much more concerned with the actual process of decision making. Many of the more sophisticated models of political scientists are models of decision making under uncertainty as applied to representatives who want to be reelected but are uncertain of the stand their constituencies might take on some issue. The actual decision-making process is an area we have entirely ignored, perhaps because of our training as

until recatly

economists. In analyzing the theory of the firm, for example, most economists simply assume that the firm will be able to achieve its goal (usually assumed to be profit maximization); they do not examine the process by which the goal is achieved. Economists generally focus on the implications of profit maximization rather than on the methods. We have made an analogous assumption — namely, that congressional representatives desire to get elected (a basically Downsian assumption) and that the representatives we observe are those who are rather good at making decisions that enable them to get elected. The market for elected representatives is a competitive market, and the people we observe are those who have been successful in coming up with the optimal strategy. Thus, our argument is comparable to that of Alchian (1950), who maintains that the firms we observe in reality are the firms that have been able to make optimal decisions, whether or not they understand the nature of the decisions. We have made a similar assumption about members of Congress: Once we analyzed what an optimal strategy would entail, we assumed that individuals who had been elected were those who had adopted this strategy.

Another distinguishing characteristic of our work is our complete reliance on published objective data rather than on interview data, which is so heavily relied upon by most political scientists. Economists generally feel more comfortable with observed behavior rather than with explanations of behavior — that is, they feel that individuals are able to behave optimally but are not necessarily able to explain why they behaved as they did. This reliance upon observed behavior goes back to the debates in the 1940s about the behavior of firms.

For politicians, the observed behavior we examine is what Nozick (1974) calls a *filter mechanism*. The congressional representatives whom we have observed have, in a sense, passed through a filter — that is, they have behaved in ways that have enabled them to be elected. It is not necessarily (or even probably) true that they understand the details of the filter mechanism, so asking them why they behave as they do would not necessarily produce any useful information. For example, consider the issue of ideology: Possibly only representatives who share a certain ideology with the majority of their constituents can be elected from a given district. If so, asking whether representatives speak for their districts or vote from the viewpoint of personal ideology is a meaningless question; a representative's ideology will be the same as the prevailing ideology of his or her district. Moreover, if asked directly, a representative may claim to ignore constituents in making decisions, but this claim is also irrelevant. In fact, we find in part II that we get essentially identical results whether we represent ideology in terms of the Americans for Democratic Action rating of a representative's voting positions (a measure of a representative's personal ideology) or in terms of the Ford-Carter or Nixon-McGovern vote in the representative's district (a measure of constituent ideology).

Similar arguments about significant variables might be applied to research such as that of Matthews and Stimson (1975), who are able to predict roll call votes quite well by examining only the voting of "cue setters" — that is, of figures who provide information for particular representatives. Matthews and Stimson use these results to imply that members of Congress may not be representing their districts. However, a representative is able to choose from among large numbers of potential cue setters in Congress. A representative from a liberal district who chose a conservative cue setter probably would not be reelected, but a representative elected from a liberal district would probably not want to choose a conservative cue setter in the first place. Thus, the fact that Matthews and Stimson are able to explain a high percentage of congressional voting without even examining district data does not mean that constituent influences are lacking in effect on congressional voting habits. Fiorina (1974) makes a similar point in his critique of earlier studies that relied on party as an explanatory variable; he says that a district with certain characteristics will elect a Republican representative who will then vote Republican, but the fact that party affiliation explains his or her vote does not mean the representative is not representing his or her constituency. Our point is the same as Fiorina's, but generalized: Most of the variables that political scientists have used to explain roll call voting may be secondary variables and constituent characteristics the primary variable. In part II we use no data internal to Congress (e.g., the vote of opinion leaders on an issue) to explain voting.

Another way in which our model differs from those used by political scientists is that our model is substantially more complete: We consider not only the effect of constituency characteristics on voting decisions but also the impact of contributions to electoral campaigns — a fact that should not be taken as a criticism of the political science models since the statistical tools and the data required for including contributions in the analysis have only recently been developed. (The data on contributions has only recently been produced by the Federal Elections Commission.) Nonetheless, we are not aware of any other instance in the literature of a model that allows for the effects on congressional voting of constituent characteristics and campaign contributions, as well as for the effects on constituent voting and on campaign contributions of the voting decisions of members of Congress.

The role of contributions in political campaigns has been studied both by political scientists and by economists. One important source is Alexander (1979). Abrams and Settle (1978) have also written on campaign finance, as has Palda (1975). Another source which is in the spirit of our analysis of campaign contributions is Jacobson (1980), who examines in detail the spending decisions of incumbents and challengers. He concludes that challengers spend all they can and that more competent challengers (or challengers facing incumbents who are less strong) are able to raise more money than are less competent challengers. Incumbents raise all the money they want; they raise more money if opposed by strong challengers. Thus, Jacobson finds that the amount of money spent by the incumbent and the amount spent by the challenger are both negatively associated with the share of the vote received by the incumbent.

In one sense Jacobson's model is incomplete, as is our own model in the same dimension. If it were possible to control fully for the strength of the challenger relative to the strength of the incumbent before the election, more spending by the incumbent would probably increase the margin of the incumbent. What we observe is that the challenger who is relatively more powerful than the incumbent raises more money and also forces the incumbent to raise more money. The incumbent, however, is unable to overcome the effect of the strong challenger, so that the share of the vote received by the incumbent is negatively associated with his or her spending. This conclusion — a result of Jacobson's model as well as of ours — is thus a statistical artifact created by the lack of any good data on relative strength prior to political campaigns.

A GENERAL EQUILIBRIUM MODEL OF CONGRESSIONAL VOTING

In part II we test several models of voting behavior. The model tested in chapter 7 is a complete model of the behavior of all the actors in the congressional system. Though it is explicitly tested only in the later chapter, we must discuss this simultaneous model here since it is the theoretical underpinning of all the empirical results described below.

Our model includes three classes of agents: members of Congress, constituents, and contributors to congressional campaigns. In all cases, the behavior of the agents is simultaneously determined. Members of Congress vote as their constituents desire, since the vote received by a member is a function of how closely his or her vote follows the desires of constituents. Similarly, members of Congress want money to help them be reelected. This money comes from contributors, who give to members of Congress who vote as the contributors desire. Members of Congress may also change their votes in response to contributors' desires. Moreover, as we saw earlier, the opponent is also an important element of this system: Incumbent members of Congress with stronger opponents receive lower electoral margins from their constituents and also are forced to raise and spend more money in order to be reelected. Note that we do not ask which of these elements is "first" or most important; rather, the model (both the theoretical model and the empirical model) is formulated simultaneously; we examine all the relationships together.

The actions of the three classes of agents in our model are the outcome of a dynamic bargaining process in discrete time. We assume that each class of agents has accurate knowledge about the proposed actions of that class. (The following material is highly technical; some readers may wish to skip to the summary at the end of this chapter.)

The means by which members of Congress, constituents, and contributors pursue their goals are by voting on bills, $\bar{V}$, voting in elections, M, and making campaign contributions, $\bar{F}$, respectively. We ignore the problem of the voters' paradox and take as an observation the fact that voters act as if their individual votes count. The voters' paradox may be explained in part by the organization of voters into interest groups that influence their members to vote. A number of such interest groups will appear as exogenous variables, $\bar{I}$, in the structural model to be tested.

The objective of a congressional representative we allow to be almost completely general. Of course, we expect the representative to be primarily concerned with the electoral margin, M, but also, perhaps, with his or her voting platform, $\bar{V}$, beyond its effect on constituents and contributors. In addition, a representative may care about contributions, $\bar{F}$, beyond their effect on the electoral outcome. The other possible influences a representative might consider would be the vector, $\bar{I}$, of constituent characteristics or the vector, $\bar{S}$, of his or her own characteristics (seniority and party). In all, then, the objective of a member of Congress is expressed as some $\phi(M, \bar{F}, \bar{V}, \bar{I}, \bar{S})$.

The contributors' objective is to have their representatives vote for bills in a way advantageous to them. Because we treat only actual representatives and not all candidates, our model emphasizes actions by contributors aimed at influencing representatives' decisions rather than actions aimed at assuring representatives' elections. The latter consideration could be handled by entering M into the objectives of the contributors, but we assume that contributors have no accurate knowledge of what the actual margin is to be and must form expectations. We suppose that seniority, party, and the announced voting pattern of a member of Congress, along with TF and TL, the total contributions to the member and to the opponent, respectively, serve as adequate indications of whether the contributors expect the member to be elected. These entities are all the variables that determine the actual margin,

M, save for the absence of constituent characteristics, $\bar{I}$, which contributors are assumed to ignore. We will later find empirically that total loser contributions, TL, turn out to be particularly strong indicators of the margin a representative receives.

Once cost of contributions is taken into account, the objective of a contributor takes the form $\psi\,(\bar{V}, \bar{F}, \bar{S}, TL) \equiv \tilde{\psi}[\bar{V}, \bar{F}, \gamma''\,(\bar{V}, S, TF, TL)]$, where γ'' is the congressional margin, M, anticipated by the contributor. We are supposing here that contributions to each member of Congress can be considered in isolation from contributions to members in other districts.

Like contributors, constituents are interested in the voting behavior and characteristics of their district representatives. They may also take into account their own characteristics, I, or consider the electoral margin, M, directly, beyond its influence on the voting platform of a representative. In general, then, the objective of the electorate takes the form $\Theta\,(\bar{V}, M, \bar{I}, \bar{S})$.

We view actually observed behavior as the end result of an adjustment process in which agents modify their positions in light of the previously expressed positions of other agents. The representative will be thought of as having the more active role in this process; donors and voters are more passive. While none of the agents is presumed omniscient, donors and voters exhibit bounded rationality to a greater extent. In particular, they do not take one another's reactions into account, but only those of the representative. In contrast, the representative considers the reactions of both groups in choosing a course of behavior. As always, myopia need not indicate any intrinsic lack of rationality but may merely reflect the costs of acquiring information or of making complex decisions. The fact that their actions have greater personal consequences, as well as the fact that they have easier access to information about the political process, makes it plausible that representatives engage in more strategic behavior than do the other agents.

We approach our problem via reaction functions, a device familiar from oligopoly theory. We are seeking a Cournot-Nash equilibrium, though not in the narrow sense that each party chooses the best response to others' actions. Rather, we suppose that, taking other agents' past actions as given, each agent perceives his or her reply to lead to the best possible future outcome. The narrower, static interpretation of equilibrium is inappropriate in the present context since, given others' actions, one has no incentive to do anything. On the other hand, if one takes others' reaction functions, rather than actions, as given (as in the Stackelberg model), in a static setting one rapidly obtains reduced form equations — that is, a situation where decisions are based solely on exogenous parameters. We are interested, instead, in obtaining structural equations suitable for econometric testing. Such equations are provided by a dynamic framework.

Agents assume, as will turn out to be true, that the present actions of others are determined by the immediate past, so that each agent should try by present action to influence future events. These events they limit to next-period outcomes. What the present actions of the other agents are to be is not yet known when an agent must decide upon present action. Thus, representatives wish to

$$\max \phi \ (M_{t+1}, \bar{F}_t, \bar{V}_t, \bar{I}, \bar{S})$$

subject to

$$M_t' = f' \ (\bar{V}_{t-1}, \dot{M}_{t-1}', \bar{I}, \bar{S} \ )$$

$$\bar{F}_t = g' \ [\bar{V}_{t-1}, \bar{F}_{t-1}, \bar{S}, \ \lambda(M_t', \bar{F}_t, \bar{V}_t, \bar{I}, \bar{S})]$$

$$M_t = \tilde{\mu}[M_t', TF_t, \lambda(M_t', \bar{F}_t, \bar{V}_t, \bar{I}, \bar{S})] \text{ with } TF_t = \Sigma F_{i, \, t}$$

$$\equiv \mu(M_t', \bar{F}_t, \bar{V}_t, \bar{I}, \bar{S}), \tag{3.1}$$

so that, optimizing with respect to the control $\bar{V}_t$, we have

$$\bar{V}_t = h(\bar{V}_{t-1}, M_{t-1}', \bar{F}_{t-1}, \bar{I}, \bar{S}).$$

By setting $\bar{V}_t = \bar{V}_{t-1}$, equilibrium votes occur as

$$\bar{V} = \tilde{\alpha}(M', \bar{F}, \bar{I}, \bar{S}).$$

The function $\tilde{\mu}$ represents a representative's perception of what votes, M_t, he or she would actually receive in any situation, given the electorate's indicated vote, M_t'. The difficulty arises because voters do not vote as they have indicated since they do not account for the eventual effects campaigning may have on their perceptions. The variables TF and TL that a representative considers so as to anticipate voter behavior, M_t, on the basis of proposed behavior, M_t', are, in fact, the variables that alter voter behavior. Not knowing TL with any accuracy, however, a representative must estimate it. This estimation is represented by the functional form λ argument in $\tilde{\mu}$. Representatives use information about themselves, their constituents, and agents' proposed reactions to their candidacies to form expectations of financial support for their opponents. Since M_t clearly should be monotone in M_t', one can solve for $M_t' = \mu^{-1}(M_t, \bar{F}_t, \bar{V}_t, \bar{I}, \bar{S})$ and express equilibrium votes as $\bar{V} = \alpha(M, \bar{F}, \bar{I}, \bar{S})$. Whereas M' is the equilibrium planned voting by the electorate, M is the actual voting anticipated by the representative in equilibrium. The reaction functions for the other agents as perceived by the representative, f' and g', are of the same structural form as the actual ones will be seen to be when one recalls that λ is the representative's expectations of TL. In particular, they may be the correct ones. It will be assumed that, in equilibrium at least, the representative, as the winner, correctly predicts the actual margin, given the indicated one.

Now contributor i wishes to

$$\max \psi_i(\overline{V}_{t+1}, \overline{F}_t, \overline{S}, TL)$$

subject to

$$\overline{V}_t = h''(\overline{V}_{t-1}, \overline{F}_{t-1}, \overline{S})$$

$$F_{j, t} = g_j''(\overline{V}_{t-1}, \overline{F}_{t-1}, \overline{S}, TL) \qquad j \neq i,$$

so that

$$F_{i, t} = g_i(\overline{V}_{t-1}, \overline{F}_{t-1}, \overline{S}, TL),$$

and equilibrium contributions occur as

$$\overline{F} = \beta(\overline{V}, \overline{S}, TL). \tag{3.2}$$

Note that each contributor foresees other contributors reacting as he or she does. We have already seen that contributors consider the effect of their actions on representatives but suppress the influence of a representative's constituency.

Finally, voters wish to

$$\max \theta(\overline{V}_{t+1}, M_t', \overline{I}, \overline{S})$$

subject to

$$\overline{V}_t = h'''(\overline{V}_{t-1}, M_{t-1}', \overline{I}, \overline{S}),$$

so that

$$M_t' = f(\overline{V}_{t-1}, M_{t-1}', \overline{I}, \overline{S}).$$

Solving for equilibrium planned electoral margin, one obtains

$$M' = \tilde{\gamma}(\overline{V}, \overline{I}, \overline{S}). \tag{3.3}$$

In addition to its indirect appearance through h''' or θ, $\overline{I}$ appears directly as an index of the distribution of voter characteristics in the aggregation of individual voters into electoral margins. Contributors have not been included in h''' in accordance with our presumption that, while voters consider the effect of their actions on representatives, they ignore the effect of the donors. However, total contributions, $TF = \Sigma F_i$, reappear in the actual behavior of voters as a result of the election campaign affecting their planned vote, as do total loser contributions, TL.

This effect, which is anticipated by representatives in μ, explains why representatives, while primarily interested in electoral margins, give consideration to contributors. Actual contributions are not forthcoming until after the bargaining process between agents has been completed. It would not have been appropriate to include consideration of this effect in the response function, f, since voters, even if they do anticipate some such influence, may, in view of their bounded rationality, be viewed as having little prior notion as to the outcome of the effect and little incentive to consider the complication further.

Including this actual effect, we obtain

$$M = \gamma(\overline{V}, \overline{I}, \overline{S}, TF, TL),$$

where M is not the indicated but the actual electoral margin. In review, we obtain as a model to be tested the equilibrium equations

$$\overline{V} = \alpha(M, \overline{F}, \overline{I}, \overline{S}),$$
$$\overline{F} = \beta(\overline{V}, \overline{S}, TL),$$
$$M = \gamma(\overline{V}, \overline{I}, \overline{S}, TF, TL), \tag{3.4}$$

where we have the following endogenous variables:

$\overline{V}$ (vector of congressional votes);

$\overline{F}$ (vector of contributions, with $TF = \Sigma F_i$);

M (electoral margin);

we also have the following exogenous variables:

$\overline{I}$ (vector of constituent characteristics);

$\overline{S}$ (vector of congressional characteristics, both seniority and party);

TL (total contributions to the losing candidate).

The above equilibrium system has a solution (V^*, F^*, M^*) when there is a dynamic solution $(V^*, F^*, M^{*\prime})$ to

$$M_t' = f(\overline{V}_{t-1}, M_{t-1}', \overline{I}, \overline{S}),$$
$$\overline{F}_t = g(\overline{V}_{t-1}, \overline{F}_{t-1}, \overline{S}, TL),$$
$$\overline{V}_t = h(\overline{V}_{t-1}, M_{t-1}', \overline{F}_{t-1}, \overline{I}, \overline{S}). \tag{3.5}$$

This is so since, by assumption,

$$\mu(M^{*\prime}, \overline{F}^*, \overline{V}^*, \overline{I}, \overline{S}) = M^* \text{ or } \mu^{-1}(M^*, \overline{F}^*, \overline{V}^*, \overline{I}, \overline{S}) = M^{*\prime}.$$

On the basis of the last period's proposed positions, agents indicate what position they prefer to take in the present period. Revelation of proposed constituents' support is expedited by polls and other surveys. The process ends only when a consistent set of $\overline{V}$, M, and $\overline{F}$ has been found. These solve (3.4) and form an equilibrium situation in the sense that no agent wishes to alter his or her behavior in view of the anticipated response of others. Note that, even so, such equilibria are not in general assured to be Pareto optimal. It is presumed that actually observed behavior represents such an equilibrium because it is the result of previous, unobserved negotiations among agents.

We are, of course, interested in whether we can expect this process to have a resting point and whether it will occur. In order to proceed we make explicit the assumption that representatives are allowed to pursue mixed strategies, so that, besides the possibilities of voting for or against a bill, they may instead propose to vote in either of the two ways according to certain probabilities. This option seems particularly appropriate when one realizes that bills seldom represent the precise position the representative would wish to take or to oppose. This convexification of the strategy space is much like what happens in using the logit analysis in the econometric analysis to follow. It further allows for the usual fixed points arguments, such as the celebrated one assuring a Nash equilibrium (Nash 1950). However, since we wish to have global stability in addition, we will instead rely on the stronger contraction mapping principle (Luenberger 1969).

Define $\varrho = f \times g \times h$; then the domain A of this mapping may be considered closed. We suppose that ϱ is a contraction — that is, it has the property that $\|\varrho(x) - \varrho(y)\| \leq \alpha \|x - y\|$ for some $\alpha < 1$ and for all x, y in A. In this case, ϱ has a fixed point obtained by the iteration of ϱ. This condition occurs when, considering any two positions of an agent, he or she takes up positions proportionately nearer after a round of negotiations than previously. It is assured by the mean value theorem when $\| D\varrho \| \leq \alpha < 1$ over the entire domain. For instance, considering the max norm

$$\|x\| = \max_i | x_i |,$$

if $D\varrho$ is dominant diagonal, and for each component

$$\left| \frac{\partial \varrho_i}{\partial x_i} \right| \leq \beta < \frac{1}{2} \text{ over all } A,$$

then ϱ is a contraction mapping. In the situation where the adjustment mechanism is contracting, there will be exactly one overall agreement, and it will be attained.

*   *   *

To summarize: Roll call voting has mainly been studied by political scientists, who have been primarily concerned with the nature of democratic decision making. In contrast, we are concerned with the nature of the forces that determine which laws will be passed. We assume that a relationship exists between the voting behavior of congressional representatives, the voting behavior of constituents, and the contributions of donors to campaigns. This relationship is modeled in this chapter and tested later in the text. The main purpose of our model is to demonstrate that a theoretical structure can be built that will give a simultaneous solution to the problem faced by the three classes of agents; moreover, this solution is stable. In part II we will "flesh out" the theoretical relationships we have discussed here.

II EVIDENCE

4 PUBLIC INTEREST LOBBIES

In part I we argued that ideological factors may be influential in explaining the passage of legislation. In this, the empirical section, we examine several measures of ideology in order to determine whether ideology is, in fact, important. In all cases we attempt to abstract from economic determinants of legislation in order to get a pure measure of ideology. In this chapter we examine the effects of so-called public interest lobbies on the passage of legislation. (We do not believe these organizations actually represent anything that can be called the "public interest." We believe that markets can generally do an adequate job of protecting the public.) First we examine the determinants of membership in public interest lobbies; next we examine the influence of these organizations on legislation. Holding constant the economic factors associated with voting, the size of the public interest lobbies in a given state does seem to influence the voting of that state's representatives on bills on which the lobbies take a position.

The standard economic theory of political participation by citizens (as opposed to producers) is that citizens do not participate. This theory has been developed by Olson (1965) and modified by Stigler (1974), but Stigler deals primarily with the small-number case. The theory holds that free rider problems are so severe that it does not pay for citizens to join a lobby such as Common Cause. Similarly, in the case of another form of political participation, voting, the theory holds that the probability of any one vote's influencing an election is so small that any finite cost of voting will make the act of voting not worthwhile (Downs 1957, Tullock 1967).

But people do appear to participate in political decision making. In 1976 over 40 million people voted in the presidential election (U.S. Bureau of the Census 1977). Similarly, over 250,000 people have paid at least fifteen dollars to belong to Common Cause, and over 180,000 people have contributed to Public Citizen, Ralph Nader's lobby. These statistics are puzzles in economic theory.

Voting has been intensely studied (for a recent example, see Ashenfelter and Kelley 1975). Voters do appear to respond to incentives insofar as increased costs of voting decrease voting and increased benefits from voting (in terms of the probability of influencing an election) increase voting (Barzel and Silberburg 1973). However, though citizens do respond at the margin to the costs and benefits of voting, the total cost of voting remains greater than the total benefit when benefit is measured in terms of the expected value of changing the outcome of the election. The voting decision has also been studied by political scientists: For a recent example, see Ferejohn and Fiorina (1974, 1975). However, no agreement exists among political scientists about the causes of voting; the Ferejohn and Fiorina articles, for example, generated a substantial number of comments in the *American Political Science Review* (September 1975). Thus, among both economists and political scientists the motivation for public participation in the political process is not well understood.

DETERMINANTS OF MEMBERSHIP IN
PUBLIC INTEREST LOBBIES

McFarland (1976) argues that the increasing importance of public interest lobbies in recent years is due to increasing numbers of college-educated people, growth of civic skepticism, strong leadership (e.g., prominent people like Ralph Nader and John Gardner), improved technology of communications, increased prosperity, and the fact that "initial success brings more success" — that is, once such a lobby proves its power to influence legislation, more people join the lobby. McFarland does not empirically test any of these hypotheses, and, while he discusses Olson's (1965) theory, he does not give any convincing explanation of how the free rider problem has been solved.

An alternative to viewing membership in such groups as a producer is to view it as a consumption good, the same viewpoint that is a popular explanation for citizens' voting (see Wittman 1975). While this explanation lacks the elegance of Stigler's (1971) theory of political behavior, it may nonetheless be the best explanation available. We will assume that some consumers desire to purchase a good that we will call "participation," and that one way to purchase this good is to join a citizens' lobby. Following standard procedure, we will assume tastes for participation to be constant and examine costs and benefits to determine the amount of participation that citizens will choose to buy.

On the supply side the most important change associated with membership in citizens' lobbies is probably reduced communication costs. As communication becomes cheaper, members can discuss stands on bills with each other, and lobby officials in Washington can more easily communicate with members to better coordinate letter-writing campaigns. Cheaper communications would be especially important in the case of Common Cause, which relies on telephone networks to generate letters to representatives in lobbying.

We may identify two potential demand factors. First is income; it seems reasonable to hypothesize that membership in the lobby is a normal good. The second demand factor is education. Several theoretical explanations of a relationship between membership and education are possible. It might be that education and membership are complementary inputs in producing participation with a Lancaster (1966)-type production function. Alternatively, Schumpeter's (1950) argument about the hostility of intellectuals toward capitalism may be relevant. Also, education may lower the cost of using membership to purchase participation. We are not able at this stage to distinguish between these various hypotheses, but we are able to test for the general significance of education.

To test our hypotheses, we used state data.[1] Membership based on state was obtained from both Common Cause and Public Citizen. An OLS regression was then run with per capita membership as the dependent variable and the following independent variables: Urban areas were based in the economies of scale that occur from the reduction of transport and communication costs. Thus, percentage urban in 1970 was used to measure communication costs, the supply variable. Per capita income for 1970 was used to determine if participation is a normal good. Percentage of college graduates in 1970 was used as our education measure. Voting in the 1972 election was used to ascertain whether voting and joining a lobby were complementary methods of purchasing participation. Percentage black was used to determine if a taste adjustment was useful.

Table 4.1.   Determinants of Common Cause and Public Citizen Membership

Determinant	Common Cause	Public Citizen
Constant	−10.61	−14.903
	(−1.08)	(−2.45)
% urban, 1970	0.0337	0.0375
	(1.20)	(1.76)[b]
% black	−0.0361	0.0151
	(−0.355)	(0.190)
Income per capita, 1970 pop.	.00133	0.000927
	(0.939)	(0.840)
% college graduates, 1970	1.564	0.989
	(4.45)[a]	(3.60)[a]
% voting, 1972	0.0113	0.0956
	(1.07)	(1.17)
R^2	0.592	0.521
d.f.	44.	44.

Note: t-values in parentheses.
[a]Significant at the 0.05 level.
[b]Significant at the 0.10 level.
Source: Data from U.S. Bureau of the Census (1977).

Table 4.1 shows that the only significant variable was percentage of the population with four or more years of college. Thus, going to college did influence membership in these lobbies. Urbanization was weakly significant in one case (though not for Common Cause, where we would have expected this variable to be significant). None of the other variables was significant. Thus, one of McFarland's conjectures was not falsified; his other conjectures either were rejected or were not tested because of the cross-section nature of our data. In such a cross section we had no way to test for the significance of "initial success breeding more success"; and because of the relatively short lives of the groups in question, we had no way to test his hypotheses using time series data.

To determine the relationship between membership in citizens' lobbies and voting, percentage of the population voting in the 1972 election was used in the membership equation; it was not significant. In addition, several equations were run with voting as the dependent variable and membership in Common Cause and Public Citizen, as well as standard voting variables (income, education, race, number of voters in the state, closeness of the election in the state), as independent variables. Membership in the lobbies was never significant in these equations. Thus, in terms of our specification, voting and membership do not appear to be complementary methods of purchasing participation. However, less aggregated data might possibly show a relationship.

INFLUENCE OF PUBLIC INTEREST LOBBIES — — pretty shoddy

Though we do not know much about why people contribute to citizens' lobbies, our lack of knowledge might not be significant: After all, economists neither know nor care why people buy most consumer goods. However, lobbying is aimed at changing law, and such changes are a public good (or bad). Thus, empirical evidence about the effectiveness of these lobbies, rather than the casual and anecdotal evidence we now have, becomes important.

Information about the effectiveness of public interest lobbies is important for another reason. The strength of the lobbies seems to derive from an ideological viewpoint, and the evidence that education is associated with membership in these lobbies is consistent with this view. But the role of ideology in passing legislation has recently been challenged by Stigler (1976) and Coase (1974); they argue that laws are passed by economically interested groups and that ideology is irrelevant. (Coase is less pessimistic than Stigler on this point.) Stigler and Coase cast their arguments in terms of the effectiveness of economists and economic analysis in influencing legislation; but presumably, if ideas in general can influence legislation, economic ideas can also have an influence. Conversely, if the ideologies of economists have no influence, neither would the ideas of Ralph Nader or John Gardner. Thus, if we can show that ideologically based lobbies influence legislation, we might have evidence that economists can, by changing ideas, have some influence on legislation.

To determine the effectiveness of public interest lobbies, we examined two bills on which Public Citizen had taken a stand and three bills favored by Common Cause (see the appendix to this chapter for a detailed description of the bills). Public Citizen–backed bills were Government in the Sunshine and a bill that would increase the power of state attorneys general to bring antitrust suits.[2] Common Cause–backed bills were the appropriation for the supersonic transport aircraft, the Federal Elections Campaign Act, and the Fisher amendment to an energy act.[3]

We used a special case of the full structural simultaneous equation model known as a *recursive system*. In this system the structural equations are ordered in such a way that the first equation has only one endogenous variable, and the second has two. Hence, all the variables except the dependent variable in any particular equation can be treated as predetermined. It is

Table 4.2. Determinants of Influence of Public Interest Lobbies
on Congressional Voting

Determinant	Government in the Sunshine	State Antitrust Suit Bill
Constant	−0.986	−1.046
	(1.161)	(1.178)
Common Cause members per 10,000 population	—	—
Public Citizen members per 10,000 population	−0.0678 (0.0252)ᵃ	−0.0697 (0.0253)ᵃ
% urban	−0.0109 (0.00646)ᵇ	−0.0142 (0.00702)ᵃ
% black	0.0257 (0.0167)	0.0244 (0.0169)
Income per capita	0.0000265 (0.000383)	0.0000689 (0.000397)ᵇ
% voting	−0.0171 (0.0189)	−0.0190 (0.0192)
% college graduates	0.234 (0.062)ᵃ	0.243 (0.0626)ᵃ
Dummy NS (1 = South)	0.442 (0.293)	0.429 (0.294)
Party (1 = R)	1.949 (0.178)ᵃ	1.919 (0.180)ᵃ
% auto employees	—	—
% airline employees	—	—
Oil production	—	—

ᵃSignificant at the 0.05 level for a two-tailed test.
ᵇSignificant at the 0.10 level for a two-tailed test.
Source: Data from U.S. Bureau of the Census (1977).

unnecessary with this recursive system to use a simultaneous mixed probit analysis (see Schmidt and Strauss 1976, Wold 1954).

The method of statistical analysis used for the second equation was probit analysis, with votes by individual members of Congress as the (0,1) dependent variable. The recursive results of the analysis are reported in table 4.2.

Table 4.2. Continued

Determinant	SST Bill	Federal Elections Campaign Act	Energy Tax Amendment
Constant	0.137	− 0.785	− 0.398
	(0.925)	(1.147)	(0.995)
Common Cause	0.0320	0.0771	0.114
members per	(0.0224)	(0.0274)[a]	(0.0259)[a]
10,000 population			
Public Citizen	—	—	—
members per			
10,000 population			
% urban	− 0.00579	− 0.0108	− 0.000834
	(0.00577)	(0.00694)	(0.00612)
% black	− 0.0136	0.00882	− 0.0118
	(0.0150)	(0.0163)	(0.612)
Income per	0.000209	0.000633	− 0.000538
capita	(0.000316)	(0.000373)[b]	(0.000334)
% voting	0.00907	0.0258	0.0389
	(0.0165)	(0.0197)	(0.0178)
% college	− 0.375	− 0.186	− 0.0869
graduates	(0.0636)	(0.0757)[a]	(0.0681)
Dummy NS	− 0.598	0.653	0.277
(1 = South)	(0.275)[a]	(0.356)[b]	(0.307)
Party (1 = R)	− 0.407	− 0.739	− 0.616
	(0.138)[a]	(0.176)[a]	(0.152)[a]
% auto	—	—	− 0.124
employees			(0.0513)[a]
% airline	− 0.314	—	—
employees	(0.063)[a]		
Oil production	—	—	0.0000335
			(0.0001074)

[a]Significant at the 0.05 level for a two-tailed test.
[b]Significant at the 0.10 level for a two-tailed test.
Source: Data from U.S. Bureau of the Census (1977).

The independent variables are the same variables used in table 4.1 as well as membership in the lobbies. This structure was used to determine whether membership was significant in determining voting after adjusting for the other factors. In addition, two of the bills (the SST appropriation and the Fisher amendment) could have affected various economic interests, so measures of these interests (state airline employment for the SST bill;[4] state oil production and automotive employment for the Fisher amendment) were included.[5] In addition, political party of each representative was considered (Republican = 1, Democrat = 0) since previous work (Danielsen and Rubin 1977) has shown party affiliation to be an important determinant of voting after adjustment for economic variables. Also included was a dummy North-South variable (South = 1).

The results indicate that public interest lobbies were, in fact, effective in influencing legislators' votes. In four out of five cases, the variable was significant at the 0.05 level, and in all cases the sign was correct. (Some signs are positive and some negative since the lobbies backed some bills and opposed others.) The only case in which membership in the relevant lobby was not significant was the SST appropriation. Common Cause, in promotional literature, had associated itself with this issue; however, the vote took place in 1971, when the lobby was just forming and was therefore relatively weak. It is at least plausible that the lobby claimed to have influenced the SST decision in order to give an appearance of strength that would aid recruitment. The votes in which the lobbies' influence appears to have been significant took place at later dates.

Political party affiliation was always significant and always had the sign opposite to the lobby variable. Thus, both Common Cause and Public Citizen appeared to take stands favored by Democrats and opposed by Republicans. The college graduate variable was sometimes significant and always opposite in sign to the lobby variable. While evidence we saw earlier indicates that college graduates are more likely than others to join public interest lobbies, total membership in both lobbies is, at most, 430,000 (assuming no overlap), while the total number of college graduates is approximately 16 million. Thus, most college graduates do not join either of these groups, and those graduates who do not join seem to be opposed to the stands of the lobbies.

The results of this research are somewhat surprising. For the theoretical reasons discussed earlier, we would not expect public interest lobbies to be influential in changing representatives' voting. One possible explanation is that we have omitted some significant variable that would reflect the self-interest of some group in passage of the legislation involved. However, it is not clear what interest groups would have a stake in the sorts of laws used in our research. At any rate, explaining the apparent significance of these lobbies' influence would appear to provide a challenge for students of political behavior. For example, the "liberalism" of representatives, as measured by some group such as the Americans for Democratic Action, would possibly explain some of the voting. However, while we have not examined the effect of the ADA rating, we have included party affiliation (P, democrat = 1) and region (dummy North-South, South = 1), and these two variables explain much of the variation in ADA ratings given to members of Congress. For 1974, the relationship is as follows (ADA ratings are from the *Congressional Quarterly Almanac*; t values are shown in parentheses):

$$ADA = 0.2388 - 0.30903DNS + 0.44277P \qquad r^2 = 0.55.$$
$$ (14.34) \quad (-13.04) \quad\quad (20.63)$$

In sum, the existence and power of the public interest lobbies seem to be a major puzzle for the economic theory of political behavior. To the extent that such groups are influential in passing legislation with substantial economic impacts, it is important for us to understand the sources of their power. In this chapter we have seen that membership in these public interest lobbies is strongly associated with college education and that these groups do appear to have significant impacts in influencing voting by representatives. The task of specifying a theory of membership in such groups (and a theory of political participation in general) still remains. Finally, to the extent that public interest groups are ideological in nature, their influence is evidence of the power of ideology to influence legislation.

APPENDIX

The bills examined in this chapter to determine the effectiveness of public interest lobbies are described below. All descriptions are from the *Congressional Quarterly*, various issues.

Government in the Sunshine.   Horton (R–N.Y.) amendment to the Flowers (D–Ala.) amendment in the nature of a substitute, to define agency meetings as only those gatherings convened for the purpose of conducting agency business. Adopted 204–180; R 123–14; D 81–166 (ND 30–138; SD 51–28); 28 July 1976. (The House subsequently adopted the Flowers amendment, as amended, by voice vote.) Opposed by Public Citizen.

State Antitrust Suits Bill.   Wiggins (R–Calif.) motion to recommit the bill to the Judiciary Committee with instructions to study the feasibility of increasing civil fines to deter antitrust violations. Rejected 105–223; R 103–23; D 47–199 (ND 10–159; SD 37–40); 18 March 1976. (A "yea" was a vote supporting the president's position.) Opposed by Public Citizen.

Department of Transportation Appropriations, Fiscal 1971.   Yates (D–Ill.) amendment to delete section appropriating an additional $434 million for development of the supersonic transport (SST) aircraft. Adopted by recorded teller vote 217–204; R 85–90; D 132–114 (ND 110–54; SD 22–60); 18 March 1971. (A "nay" was a vote supporting the president's position.) Supported by Common Cause.

Federal Elections Campaign Act.   Passage of the bill to provide for public financing of presidential election campaigns, impose campaign spending and contribution limits, and establish a board of supervisors to oversee and administer the law. Passed 355–18; R 136–45; D 219–3 (ND 148–0; SD 71–3); 8 August 1974. (A "nay" was a vote supporting the president's position.) Supported by Common Cause.

Energy Tax Amendment.   Fisher (D–Va.) amendment to impose a tax on each inefficient car providing fuel mileage below certain standards, as well as a tax on each manufacturer or importer whose cars provided average efficiency below certain standards. Rejected 166–235; R 35–101; D 131–134 (ND 109–79; SD 22–55); 12 June 1975. Supported by Common Cause.

NOTES

1. Data sources: for roll call voting and party, the *Congressional Quarterly*, various issues; for state oil production, the American Petroleum Institute (1975); for employment, U.S. Department of Commerce, *Regional Employment by Industry, 1940–1970*, n.d.

2. These two bills were chosen because an official of Public Citizen said that they were important interests of the group. In the case of the Government in the Sunshine bill, we actually used voting on an amendment to the act that would have served to weaken it; thus, Public Citizen would have been expected to oppose the amendment.

3. Common Cause literature claims that the SST bill and the federal campaign act were important victories for the lobby. McFarland (1976) identifies the lobby with the Fisher amendment; it would have placed a tax on energy-inefficient automobiles instead of continuing the current policy of legislating average mileage figures for all automobiles produced.

4. Approximately two-thirds of this type of employment is aircraft related.

5. Since the Fisher amendment would have replaced one rather inefficient set of controls on automobiles with another inefficient set, it is not clear how automobile producers or oil producers would have felt about this bill; we assume that these groups would have determined an appropriate position.

5 VOTING ON MINIMUM WAGES

In chapter 4 we examined the role of public interest lobbies in influencing congressional voting and concluded that the number of members of such lobbies in a state seemed significant in explaining the voting of congressional representatives from that state on issues that were important to the lobbies. If we believe that membership in public interest lobbies is determined by ideological factors, the evidence in chapter 4 is consistent with the hypothesis that ideology has an impact on congressional voting and hence on the passage of laws. In this chapter we continue the analysis of the influence of ideology on voting, but we use a different measure of ideology — namely, the rating given to representatives by the Americans for Democratic Action, a liberal pressure group. In chapter 6 we will explore the nature and significance of the ADA rating in further detail; the results presented in this chapter may be considered a preliminary test of the use of this rating to measure ideology.

The material in this chapter provides other useful information. We use voting on the issue of minimum wage laws during the years 1949-1974. Thus, while the data are less complete than data used in later chapters, this chapter provides a time series analysis — that is, we are able to examine the influence of the same set of factors over a long period of time. The fact that our results are consistent over this time period may provide some information about the temporal stability of the more complete results derived in later analyses.

Silberman and Durden (1976) have examined economic factors associated with voting by representatives on changes in the minimum wage in 1973. They have found that the number of low-wage workers in a congressional district is positively associated with voting for higher minimum wages by representatives from that district. This result is somewhat surprising; in fact, Silberman and Durden (hereafter referred to as S-D) were unable to predict a priori the sign of this variable. As Browning (1975) has shown, since the late 1960s transfers to low-income persons have substantially increased, particularly in terms of income in kind. Thus, in 1973 the losses of people who became unemployed on account of higher minimum wages may have been relatively smaller than losses in earlier periods. This decrease would have reduced the cost to low-wage workers of the "unemployment effect" (S-D 1976, p. 321) and might have served to make such workers, on the whole, more favorably disposed to passage of minimum wage laws.

In addition, the 1964 Voting Rights Act enfranchised many blacks. Blacks typically are low-paid workers; thus, they would have strong interest in minimum wage legislation. Time series analysis should enable us to determine any changes in the influence of blacks on voting by representatives and thus enable us to ascertain whether the Voting Rights Act has any influence on minimum wage legislation. The possibility of detecting such changes makes time series a useful adjunct to cross-section analysis. This chapter is a time series study of economic determinants of passage of minimum wage legislation. We also include ideological factors, which S-D did not consider in their analysis.

The econometric technique used is probit analysis. A (0,1) variable is defined over all representatives, with 0 being a vote against the minimum wage and 1 being a vote in favor. In each year we use the vote on final passage of the law rather than on amendments because this vote enables us to compare votes and influences over time. We use all years in which an actual legislated change in the minimum wage took place; we omit years such as 1973, in which minimum wages were considered but not passed. (In 1973 the increase in the minimum wage was vetoed by the president.) Thus, we have six separate votes, running from 1938 to 1974. As independent variables we use the following:[1]

Average Hourly Earnings in Manufacturing (AHE). Minimum wages increase the price of low-wage labor, and low-wage labor is a substitute for high-wage labor. Thus, high-wage workers should be in favor of minimum wages if the economic rationality theory is correct. As AHE in a state increase, we predict more support for minimum wage legislation.

Unions (U).   Union members are typically high-wage workers; unions serve as the political organization for these workers. Thus, unionization in a state should also be associated with voting for minimum wages.

Blacks (B).   Black workers tend to be overrepresented among low-wage workers and among the unemployed. To the extent that higher minimum wages are associated with higher employment, a rational, informed black would be expected to oppose minimum wages.

Party (P).   Minimum wage legislation may be a partisan issue. In addition, previous work (Danielsen and Rubin 1977) has shown political party to be an important variable affecting voting on economic issues after adjusting for economic interest. We define a dummy that takes the value 1 for a Democrat and 0 for a Republican.

Americans for Democratic Action (ADA).   The ADA, a liberal pressure group, annually rates members of Congress on the basis of their votes for a selected set of issues and derives a "liberalism" score for each. Thus, ADA may be a measure of ideology. (It is also possible that ADA serves to monitor membership in a coalition of economic interests; we examine this possibility in chapter 6.) Votes are selected by the ADA so that each year the average rating for all members of Congress will be about 50 percent; thus, the effect of this variable would not be expected to change over time, and the difficulty in interpretation of the variable should have no effect in explaining changes over time in voting on minimum wages.

We use statewide data for each of the first three variables (AHE, U, B) and individual data for each member of Congress for the last two (P, ADA). In 1938 the ADA did not exist, and average hourly earnings by state were not available; therefore, a dummy for the South is used as a proxy for these two variables in the 1938 estimate.

Our variables are somewhat different from those used by S-D (1976). The major reason for the difference is data availability: Many of their variables (e.g., contributions of unions and small business to political campaigns) were not available throughout the time period which we consider. In addition, they did not use any ideological variables. Finally, they used contributions by unions to political campaigns, and we use percentage of the labor force that belonged to unions in a given state. However, though unions can

make contributions to representatives in any state, we would expect contributions to be most effective when made to those representatives who
would be most sympathetic to the union cause — that is, representatives
from states with relatively large numbers of union members. We would
therefore not expect this difference in data to be significant.

The empirical results for 1949–1974 are reported in table 5.1.[2] Variables
ADA and AHE were significant in all years and were positively associated
with voting for minimum wages. Percentage of blacks in a state was
negatively associated with voting for minimum wages in all years and was
significant in 1949 and 1966. Political party was never significant — apparently because northern Democrats were in favor of minimum wage
legislation and southern Democrats were opposed; thus there was no net effect of party affiliation.

Unionization was never significant. However, there may be multicollinearity programs with unions and average hourly earnings: The correlation between these variables averaged 0.78. If AHE are excluded from the
probit analysis, unions become significant with larger likelihood estimates.
If unions are excluded, the likelihood estimates of AHE become larger. It is
thus a computationally impossible task to isolate the influence of unions and
of AHE. This is not a serious problem since if either AHE or unions (or
both) are significant, the conclusion is the same: Minimum wages are passed
at the behest of high-wage workers.

Since some of the data were not available for 1938, the results of this year
are not included in table 5.1. Using a North-South dummy variable (South
= 1) as a proxy, the 1938 probit equation is

$$\text{vote} = 0.186 + 3.487U - 1.168B + 0.737P - 0.915DNS,$$
$$\quad\quad\quad (0.28) \quad (1.206)^* \quad (0.92)^* \quad (0.20)^* \quad (0.25)^*$$

$-2 \times$ log of the likelihood ratio = 73.45, number of observations = 418,
*significant at the 0.05 level, one-tailed test.

The 1938 equation, with significant positive coefficients for unions and
negative coefficients for blacks and DNS, supports the hypothesis that
minimum wages are passed to benefit high-wage workers.

The likelihood estimates did not indicate any change over time. The coefficients for AHE, blacks, and ADA are remarkably consistent and indicate
little change in the impact of these variables over the twenty-five-year
period. We were unable to determine any effect of the Voting Rights Act or
of the increase in welfare payments on minimum wage legislation.[3] Our
result on wages disagrees with the result of S-D (1976): They found that low-
wage workers were associated with voting for minimum wages; we found
that higher wages were associated with voting for minimum wages and that

Table 5.1 Maximum-Likelihood Estimates Based on Probit Analysis for Determinants of Minimum Wage Voting

Year	Variable						Sample Size	$-2 \times$ Log Likelihood Ratio
	Constant	AHE	Unions (U)	Blacks (B)	ADA	Party (P)		
1949	-1.190	1.383	1.257	-1.728	1.765	-0.015	404	60.26
	(1.00)	(0.86)[a]	(1.75)	(1.34)[a]	(0.60)[b]	(0.47)		
1955	1.165	1.359	1.210	-1.606	1.965	-0.148	427	137.04
	(0.81)	(0.72)[b]	(1.72)	(1.27)	(0.58)[b]	(0.46)		
1961	-1.293	1.454	1.173	-1.535	1.971	-0.140	428	380.13
	(0.76)	(0.69)[b]	(1.72)	(1.27)	(0.58)[b]	(0.46)		
1966	-1.202	1.390	1.216	-1.666	1.895	-0.090	414	259.34
	(0.82)	(0.73)[b]	(1.72)	(1.28)[b]	(0.58)[b]	(0.46)		
1974	-1.328	1.484	1.179	-1.598	1.901	-0.081	419	104.96
	(0.77)	(0.70)[b]	(1.72)	(1.27)	(0.59)[b]	(0.46)		

Note: Standard errors in parentheses; maximum-likelihood ratio significant at the 0.01 level for all equations.

[a]Significant at 0.10 level, for one-tailed test, based on asymptotic t-ratio.

[b]Significant at 0.05 level, for one-tailed test, based on asymptotic t-ratio.

the presence of blacks (typically low-wage workers) was negatively and sometimes significantly associated with voting for minimum wages. Further research may be needed to resolve this discrepancy.

In a preliminary test of the hypotheses in this chapter, we used a time series regression for the period 1938–1974 with the dependent variables defined as 1 in a year in which the minimum wage changed and 0 for years with no change. The independent variables were all national variables: percentage of the black population over eighteen (B); percentage of the labor force unionized (U); number of northern Democrats in the House of Representatives (ND), a measure of liberalism; number of representatives from the Northeast divided by number of representatives from the Southeast (RR); and average hourly earnings in manufacturing (AHE). The equation derived from the above procedure is

$$MW = -0.394 + 0.734AHE + 0.0201U + 3.941RR$$
$$(-0.0813) \quad (2.642) \quad\quad (0.781) \quad\quad (1.502)$$
$$+ 0.00764ND - 54.244B,$$
$$(3.432) \quad\quad (-2.185)$$

$R^2 = 0.400$; t-values in parentheses.

The significant variables were AHE, ND, and B. These results are consistent with those obtained from the more elaborate procedure described earlier in this chapter; higher earnings and northern Democrats were significant in changing the minimum wage, and blacks were significant and negatively associated with such a change. Though this specification is weaker than that given earlier in the chapter, results are consistent.

Another issue of interest is the issue of the consistency of votes on amendments to a bill. Uri and Mixon (1980), for example, claim that work on voting on minimum wages is deficient because most such work looks only at the final passage of the bill. They examine voting on the minimum wage in 1977 as well as voting on several amendments to that bill. However, their analysis adds nothing useful since they invariably find that any group opposed to the final bill favors all amendments that weaken the bill, and that the converse is true for groups in favor of the bill. Unions and Democrats favor the bill and oppose all amendments; young workers, workers in low-wage industries, and small-business interests oppose the bill and favor all weakening amendments. Thus, the results of their study are consistent with our results and indicate that an examination of final passage probably produces enough information to render an examination of amendments unnecessary.

* * *

In sum, the results of our analysis are consistent with the hypothesis that ideological factors have an influence on legislation. Moreover, the results presented here also indicate that influences on voting are stable over a rather long time period — a fact that has some bearing on the results discussed in the next several chapters, which generally are for 1974 and 1978.

NOTES

1. Data sources: Union data by state for 1939 and 1953 are from Troy (1957); for 1964, 1970, and 1974 data are from the U.S. Bureau of the Census (1977). These are the only years for which these data are available. A weighted average was used to compute union membership in 1961. Number of blacks by state is available in the U.S. Bureau of the Census (1977); it is available for census years only. Weighted averages were used to compute number of blacks for the minimum wage years. The ADA ratings and party for 1950 and 1956 are from the *ADA World*; for subsequent years, these data are from the *Congressional Quarterly* for the appropriate year. Average hourly earnings in manufacturing are from the U.S. Department of Labor (1975). For a small number of states in 1949, average hourly earnings were not available; a simple average for the corresponding region was used. Roll call voting records and political party for 1938 are from the U.S. Congress (1938); for subsequent years, from the *Congressional Quarterly* for the appropriate year.

2. In some years the ADA included voting on minimum wages in the list of bills on which its rating was based. In 1961 the final vote was included; in 1949 another vote on the minimum wage issue was included; and in 1966 three minimum wage bills, not including the final vote, were used. This overlapping could create some problems; however, in 1955 and 1974 no minimum wage bills were included in the ADA rating, and the results for these years do not differ from those of the other years. Thus, inclusion of minimum wage votes does not seem to be a problem.

3. Thomas Borcherding (1977) has pointed out that we would not, in fact, expect higher welfare payments to change voting patterns: At any time, the lowest observed market wage would reflect all such transfers, and a minimum wage above this level would lead to undesired unemployment.

6 IDEOLOGY AND LOGROLLING

In chapters 4 and 5 we found that various measures of ideology (e.g., membership in public interest lobbies or ADA ratings) seem to affect voting by members of Congress. In this chapter we extend our analysis of the ratings earned by congressional representatives. First, having found close relationships among the ratings given by various types of ideological interest groups, we examine in some detail the determinants of these ratings. We then provide a further test of the effect of ratings on congressional voting and find that, after we have controlled for most economic variables, the ratings still seem important. However, ratings may merely be a measure of belonging to a logrolling coalition (for a discussion of logrolling, see Buchanan and Tullock 1962), so we test this hypothesis by examining interrelationships between various votes and find that, even after this adjustment, ideology seems to be important in explaining voting.

DETERMINANTS OF RATINGS

Each year several ideological pressure groups compile ratings of congressional representatives by picking a set of votes and determining a desirable

63

Table 6.1.   Correlations of Congressional
Ratings, 1973

Groups	ADA	COPE	NFU	ACA
ADA	—	—	—	—
COPE	0.850[a]	—	—	—
NFU	0.715[a]	0.819[a]	—	—
ACA	−0.897[a]	−0.891[a]	−0.800[a]	—

[a]Significant at the 0.01 level.
Source: Data from *Congressional Quarterly Almanac* (1974).

stand on each vote. Each representative is then given a rating based on the percentage of times his or her vote agreed with the preferred position of the group. Major liberal groups performing this rating function are the Americans for Democratic Action (ADA), the AFL-CIO Committee on Political Education (COPE), and the National Farm Union (NFU). One conservative rating group is the Americans for Constitutional Action (ACA). The ADA picks votes so that the average rating earned by all representatives is about 0.5; thus, such ratings as the ADA's are not suitable for a time series study by liberalism. This is consistent with Riker's (1962) contention that groups will seek a minimum winning coalition so that gains will be split among the smallest possible group of winners.

We have used ADA ratings as our first measure of ideology. Table 6.1 shows that correlations between ratings given by the various interest groups

Table 6.2.   Determinants of ADA Ratings, OLS Regressions, 1973
(Sample Size 435)

Variables	Constant	Per Capita Income	Central City Residents	% Union Members	Consumers	% Black	Hew Spending	Education
ADA1	−20.542	0.00045	0.315	0.533	1.408	0.0971	0.0158	−2.035
	(−0.60)	(0.36)	(5.85)[a]	(2.49)[a]	(1.96)[a]	(0.76)	(0.75)	(−0.85)
ADA2	44.880	0.00092	0.279	−0.261	−0.069	0.199	0.037	−5.494
	(1.22)	(0.73)	(5.22)[a]	(−0.96)	(−0.09)	(1.56)	(1.76)[b]	(2.22)[a]
ADA3	−78.928	0.00177	0.182	0.331	2.085	0.0231	−0.0089	3.317
	(−3.01)	(1.83)[b]	(4.40)[a]	(2.04)[a]	(3.82)[a]	(0.24)	(−0.57)	(1.80)[b]
ADA4	−20.30	0.0022	0.151	−0.371	0.769	0.114	0.010	0.191
	(−0.73)	(2.30)[a]	(3.73)[a]	(−1.82)[b]	(1.32)	(1.20)	(0.64)	(0.10)

Note: *t*-values in parentheses.
[a]Significant at the 0.05 level for a two-tailed test.
[b]Significant at the 0.10 level for a two-tailed test.

are quite high, so that the choice of a particular index is rather arbitrary. We refer to ADA ratings as a measure of liberalism, but everything we say could also refer, in reverse, to conservatism.[1]

We are interested in a pure measure of ideology. However, many of the votes on which the ADA bases its ratings are economic in nature. For example, many votes deal with issues of interest to unions, which are an important element in the ADA. As a first step, we regressed ADA ratings as the dependent variable on several economic independent variables. Note that at this point we are not testing any hypotheses; we have no formal theory about which interest groups are associated with liberalism. The purpose of the regression is purely to measure which groups are so associated. The economic variables follow. Note that some variables are statewide and some are for congressional districts. We use the same variables throughout this chapter.[2]

Income: per capita income in the representative's district;
Central City: percentage of residents in the representative's district who reside in a central city;
Union: percentage of residents in the representative's state who belong to unions;
Consumers: percentage of residents in the representative's state who subscribe to *Consumer Reports*;
Blacks: percentage of blacks in the representative's district;
HEW: per capita spending in the representative's district by the Department of Health, Education, and Welfare;

Table 6.2.   Continued

Age	% Farmers	Oil Production	Coal Production	DOD/P	DNS	Party	$\bar{R}^2$
0.968	−0.324	−0.0021	−0.00005	0.00058	—	—	0.22
(1.69)[b]	(−0.71)	(−1.16)	(−0.97)	(0.10)			
1.058	−0.824	0.00041	−0.00003	0.0016	−29.097	—	0.25
(1.89)[b]	(−1.78)[b]	(0.22)	(−0.53)	(0.29)	(−4.52)[a]		
0.308	0.0290	−0.0047	0.00002	−0.0056	—	42.88	0.55
(0.71)	(0.83)	(−3.40)[a]	(0.54)	(−1.31)		(17.91)[a]	
0.395	−0.161	−0.0024	0.00005	−0.0047	−25.79	42.41	0.58
(0.94)	(−0.46)	(−1.73)[b]	(1.07)	(−1.12)	(−5.36)[a]	(18.28)[a]	

Education: average level of education of residents in the representatives's district;

Age: average age of those over eighteen in the representative's district;

Farm: percentage of farmers in the representative's district;

Oil: oil production in the representative's state;

Coal: coal production in the representative's state;

DOD: per capita spending in the representative's district by the Department of Defense.

We also considered using a North-South variable as well as a political party variable. Four specifications of the ratings equation were tested; the results are reported in table 6.2, which shows that the significant variables in explaining liberalism as defined by the ADA are income, central city residents, unions, consumers, and education; oil production is significant and negative. The significance of education is consistent with Schumpeter's (1950) hypothesis, discussed in chapter 2.

ANALYSIS OF VOTES: LOGIT MODEL

We used twenty-six votes from 1974 as our sample (see table 6.3). We selected these votes from the entire set of votes for 1974 to represent as many issues as seemed feasible; we were constrained by the necessity of having some variability in the vote in order for statistical analysis to be meaningful. We included nine votes dealing with urban issues in order to look for patterns in votes dealing with similar issues. In addition to urban issues, we included votes on school busing (two), coal mining and energy (one each), HEW appropriations (one), public jobs (one), rice subsidies (two), and one vote each on defense spending, size of the national debt, civil service annuities, the proposed Consumer Protection Agency, minimum wages, the Campaign Spending Act, the Occupational Safety and Health Administration appropriation, capital punishment for airline hijackers, and environmental education. Our ADA equation was estimated for 1973 and the relevant votes are for 1974, so that we have information on the same representatives, but none of the votes studied was used in constructing the ratings equation. The ADA rating is constructed on the basis of votes, and the dependent variable is also a vote variable. However, we attempted to eliminate any influence that this factor may have had. First, our ADA variable is for a different year than the votes used. Second, we included many votes that were not directly relevant to ADA ratings (which were based on a smaller set of votes than those we included). We believe these factors mean that ADA was actually measuring something other than voting behavior — namely, ideology. The ADA variable was associated with representatives; an alternative (detailed in chapter 7) is to use some measure of ideology associated with constituents — for example, the percentage of votes for Richard Nixon in the 1972 presidential election. The correlation between this measure and ADA is -0.69.

To the extent that ADA does measure economic influence, including ADA in equations where the economic variables are already present may result in multicollinearity. Leaving ADA out would lead to the improper exclusion of ideology. Our solution was to replace ADA with another variable, RADA, that was orthogonal to the economic variables. We obtained this new variable by subtracting from the actual values of ADA the computed values obtained from the ratings equations. The observations on RADA are the residuals. This residualization technique was used by Ridker and Henning (1967) and derived from Goldberger (1964). This procedure eliminated multicollinearity between ADA and the economic variables. The coefficients of the economic variables are the same as they would have been had ADA not been included. The coefficient of RADA is unaffected by this procedure. It is, of course, possible that we have omitted economic variables from the specifications in table 6.2; this problem always exists in empirical work. However, the residualization technique does not amplify this problem. The problem of a potentially omitted variable would exist even if we had used ADA ratings without the residualization technique.

We used specification 3 from table 6.2 (in which we included party but omitted the North-South dummy variable) in constructing the residual. We chose to include party since we felt that some votes would be determined on the basis of party loyalty; therefore, this variable should be included to eliminate self-interest from the ratings. However, we felt that the difference between North and South that remained after removing economic variables was a pure ideological difference and should not be removed from our measure of ideology.

In all cases we used logit analysis. We defined a vote for a bill as 1; a vote against, 0. We counted all voting representatives, as well as representatives who were paired for or against a bill. Because statistical procedures were greatly simplified by having the same sample size for all votes, we took all representatives abstaining on a vote and assigned them either for or against the bill in accordance with the vote of the majority of voting representatives from their state. Where a tie made this procedure impossible, we used a random process. The number of representatives voting on the bills ranged from 331 to 415, with an average of 389; thus, since about 90 percent of the 435 representatives voted on the bills, we did not feel that this procedure

Table 6.3. Description of Bills Used in Logit Model

| Bill | Date of Vote | Total House Vote | | Vote by Party | | Vote by Region | |
		For	Against	Republicans	Democrats	Northern Democrats	Southern Democrats
HR 15580 (prohibit busing) Labor-HEW Appr. Fiscal 1975	June 27, 1974	231	137	126-40	105-97	47-85	58-12
HR 69 (prohibit busing) Elem. & Sec. Educ. Act Amend.	March 26, 1974	293	117	148-29	145-88	73-80	72-8
HR 10294 Land Use Planning	June 11, 1974	204	211	46-136	158-75	133-21	25-54
HR 8825 (planning grants) HUD, Space, Veterans Appr. Fiscal 1974	June 22, 1973	168	184	39-117	129-67	104-27	25-40
HR 15361 (low-interest loans housing) Housing & Community Development	June 20, 1974	274	112	116-51	158-61	119-27	39-34
HR 8825 (urban renewal) HUD, Space, Veterans Appr. Fiscal 1974	June 22, 1973	106	241	5-149	101-92	92-35	9-57
H. Jt. Resolution 512 Insured Housing Loans	Sept. 5, 1973	202[b]	172[b]	161-14	41-158	6-128	35-30
HR 8346 Nat'l. Building Standards Act	Oct. 15, 1973	108[a]	258[a]	18-149	90-109	78-47	12-62

Bill	Date						
S 502 Federal-Aid Highway Program	April 19, 1973	190	215	70–114	120–101	112–33	8–68
S 386 Urban-Mass Transit Subsidies	July 30, 1974	221^b	181^b	138–39	83–142	31–122	52–20
HR 15361 (housing subsidies) Housing & Community Development	June 20, 1974	285	114	136–38	149–76	110–39	39–37
HR 11500 Surface Mining	July 18, 1974	156	255	103–82	53–173	16–135	37–38
HR 3927 Environmental Education	Oct. 24, 1973	335	60	126–45	209–15	140–3	69–12
HR 15580 (HEW increase: CETA) Labor-HEW Appr. Fiscal 1975	June 27, 1974	231	171	47–130	184–41	144–6	40–35
HR 15580 (OSHA decrease) Labor-HEW Appr. Fiscal 1975	June 27, 1974	179	218	126–49	53–169	6–141	47–28
HR 14013 (public jobs) Supplemental Appr. Fiscal 1974	April 10, 1974	236	168	58–124	178–44	142–5	36–39
HR 12565 (increase aid to South Vietnam) Defense Supp. Authr. Fiscal 1974	April 4, 1974	154	177	99–50	55–127	19–103	36–24
HR 14832 Debt Limit Increase	May 23, 1974	191	190	75–93	116–97	77–62	39–35
S 628 Civil Service Annuity	April 24, 1974	296	102	105–71	191–31	141–8	50–23

Table 6.3. Continued

| Bill | Date of Vote | Total House Vote | | Vote by Party | | Vote by Region | |
		For	Against	Republicans	Democrats	Northern Democrats	Southern Democrats
HR 13163 Consumer Protection Agency	April 3, 1974	149[c]	241[c]	110-58	39-183	3-145	36-38
S 2747 Minimum Wage Increase	March 28, 1974	345	50	135-40	210-10	143-1	67-9
HR 16090 Federal Elections Campaign Act	Aug. 8, 1974	355	48	136-45	219-3	148-0	71-3
HR 15263 Rice Production	Dec. 17, 1974	118[d]	263[d]	84-85	34-178	22-112	12-66
HR 15263 Rice Production	Dec. 17, 1974	256	135	137-36	119-99	97-43	22-56
HR 3858 (eliminate death penalty) Anti-Hijacking Act	March 13, 1974	121	286	31-150	90-136	80-69	10-67
S 2589 (price of domestic crude oil) Nat'l. Energy Emergency Act	Feb. 27, 1974	173	238	114-65	59-173	21-131	38-42

[a]Two-thirds majority vote needed for passage.
[b]Motion to recommit bill to conference committee.
[c]Substitute amendment.
[d]Final vote on bill.
Source: *Congressional Quarterly Almanac* (1973, 1974).

would bias the results. In addition to the ideological variable (RADA), all the economic variables discussed were used except income. We omitted income because of multicollinearity problems between income and education; its inclusion does not significantly change the results but does make them more difficult to interpret.

The results of the analysis are reported in table 6.4, which shows, first (and most importantly for the hypothesis being tested), that in all cases but two the ideological variable is significant. Note that we have adjusted for economic interests by including them in the voting equation. Even with this substantial effort at removing all economic factors, we still find that ideology is significant in explaining voting.

Second, the results shown in table 6.4 indicate rather strongly the existence of a liberal coalition in Congress. This coalition seems to be made up of residents of central cities, union members, and people with an interest in consumer affairs. These three variables and RADA have the same sign in almost all cases where they are significant; in only two areas does disagreement appear. The results also give evidence of a conservative coalition consisting of farmers, oil producers, coal producers, and (to a small degree) the educated. However, evidence about a conservative coalition is more mixed and weaker than evidence about a liberal coalition.

Third, table 6.4 shows that the education variable is often opposite in sign to the RADA variable. In the regression used to determine the RADA, education had a positive sign. These two facts are consistent with an argument that a split exists within the educated segment of the population: Some well-educated people support liberal causes, and other well-educated people are opposed. This finding agrees with an earlier finding (see chapter 4) — namely, that the number of college graduates in a state is positively associated with membership in Common Cause and in Public Citizen, two public interest lobbies, but that the number of college graduates in a state is negatively related to stands taken by these lobbies. Both of these pieces of evidence are consistent with Schumpeter's (1950) hypothesis; educated citizens who are associated with liberalism could be Schumpeter's "intellectuals." To further examine this hypothesis, we would need data on the types of education citizens in various states have received.

One somewhat surprising result of our analysis was the general insignificance of the government-spending variables: HEW spending was significant in only four cases, and DOD spending was significant only three times. Furthermore, DOD spending was not significant on the bill relating to defense spending, and HEW spending was not significant on the bills relating to HEW appropriations. DOD spending was significant on the bill dealing with civil service annuities, but neither measure was significant on

Table 6.4. Logit Estimates of Congressional Votes, 1974

		Coefficient of				
Votes	*Constant*	*Central City Residents*	*% Union Members*	*Consumers*	*RADA*	*% Black*
Prohibit busing	6.358 (1.81)[b]	−0.023 (−4.75)[a]	−0.067 (−3.48)[a]	−0.157 (−2.50)[a]	−0.058 (−8.33)[a]	−0.008 (−0.72)
Prohibit busing	2.560 (0.63)	−0.028 (−5.29)[a]	−0.084 (−3.81)[a]	−0.143 (−2.01)[a]	−0.067 (−8.48)[a]	−0.016 (−1.38)
Land use planning	−1.076 (−0.34)	0.023 (4.42)[a]	0.046 (2.47)[a]	0.080 (1.27)	0.062 (8.48)[a]	−0.015 (−1.26)
Planning grants	3.953 (1.32)	0.025 (4.97)[a]	0.038 (2.27)[a]	0.150 (2.54)[a]	0.030 (5.28)[a]	0.024 (1.97)[a]
Low-interest loans housing	−0.936 (−0.33)	0.003 (0.65)	0.033 (1.92)[b]	0.192 (3.22)[a]	0.028 (4.79)[a]	0.007 (0.70)
Urban renewal	−0.810 (−0.23)	0.024 (4.83)[a]	0.016 (0.83)	0.279 (4.17)[a]	0.036 (5.72)[a]	0.015 (1.26)
Insured housing	−1.064 (−0.34)	−0.026 (−5.13)[a]	−0.059 (−3.23)[a]	−0.092 (−1.53)	−0.046 (−7.26)[a]	0.0058 (0.49)
Building standards	5.502 (1.61)[b]	0.015 (3.17)[a]	0.062 (3.29)[a]	0.015 (0.24)	0.041 (6.40)[a]	−0.020 (−1.79)[b]
Highway program	−24.197 (−4.29)[a]	0.034 (4.78)[a]	0.086 (3.63)[a]	0.368 (4.24)[a]	0.076 (7.72)[a]	0.021 (1.26)
Mass transit	3.605 (1.15)	−0.019 (−3.77)[a]	−0.063 (−3.54)[a]	−0.274 (−4.40)[a]	−0.035 (−5.91)[a]	−0.014 (−1.16)
Housing subsidies	−3.027 (−1.06)	0.005 (1.14)	−0.028 (−1.66)[b]	0.219 (3.69)[a]	0.018 (3.31)[a]	0.015 (1.42)
Surface mining	2.770 (0.95)	−0.015 (−3.03)[a]	−0.035 (−1.92)[b]	−0.150 (−2.41)[a]	−0.057 (−8.00)[a]	−0.007 (−0.65)
Environmental education	−0.496 (−0.13)	0.026 (3.49)[a]	−0.007 (−0.30)	0.107 (1.39)	0.037 (4.65)[a]	−0.017 (−1.23)
HEW increase	0.677 (0.23)	0.028 (5.07)[a]	0.065 (3.65)[a]	0.166 (2.73)[a]	0.047 (7.31)[a]	0.016 (1.30)
OSHA decrease	4.612 (1.44)	−0.026 (−4.77)[a]	−0.092 (−4.72)[a]	−0.172 (−2.63)[a]	−0.063 (−8.22)[a]	−0.002 (−0.18)
Public jobs	−0.053 (−0.01)	0.028 (4.99)[a]	0.097 (5.07)[a]	0.092 (1.46)	0.056 (7.98)[a]	0.012 (0.95)

Table 6.4. Continued

<table>
<tr><td colspan="7" align="center">Coefficient of</td><td rowspan="3">Likeli-hood Ratio Test</td></tr>
<tr><td>HEW Spending</td><td>Education</td><td>Age</td><td>% Farmers</td><td>Oil Production</td><td>Coal Production</td><td>DOD Spending</td></tr>
<tr><td>-0.002
(-1.31)</td><td>-0.326
(-1.71)[b]</td><td>0.070
(1.32)</td><td>-0.089
(-2.53)[a]</td><td>0.0002
(0.76)</td><td>0.000
(-1.19)</td><td>0.0003
(0.52)</td><td>176.8</td></tr>
<tr><td>0.0001
(0.04)</td><td>-0.264
(-1.24)</td><td>0.152
(2.36)[a]</td><td>-0.147
(-3.81)[a]</td><td>0.0001
(0.53)</td><td>0.00000
(0.65)</td><td>0.001
(1.22)</td><td>178.2</td></tr>
<tr><td>0.002
(1.29)</td><td>-0.188
(-1.04)</td><td>0.023
(0.43)</td><td>-0.123
(-3.21)[a]</td><td>-0.0005
(-2.84)[a]</td><td>-0.00001
(-2.09)[a]</td><td>-0.0004
(-0.73)</td><td>207.8</td></tr>
<tr><td>-0.001
(-0.73)</td><td>-0.516
(-2.93)[a]</td><td>0.009
(0.20)</td><td>-0.094
(-2.58)[a]</td><td>-0.0003
(-2.11)[a]</td><td>-0.00002
(-3.81)[a]</td><td>-0.001
(-2.19)[a]</td><td>150.8</td></tr>
<tr><td>0.001
(0.54)</td><td>-0.220
(-1.34)</td><td>0.035
(0.72)</td><td>0.040
(1.18)</td><td>-0.001
(-1.30)</td><td>0.000
(-0.41)</td><td>0.562
(1.19)</td><td>68.9</td></tr>
<tr><td>0.001
(0.54)</td><td>-0.385
(-1.90)[b]</td><td>0.026
(0.48)</td><td>-0.096
(-2.04)[a]</td><td>-0.0005
(-1.99)[a]</td><td>-0.0000
(-0.95)</td><td>-0.001
(-1.40)</td><td>169.5</td></tr>
<tr><td>-0.005
(-2.55)[a]</td><td>0.728
(3.82)[a]</td><td>-0.062
(-1.23)</td><td>0.039
(1.08)</td><td>-0.0003
(-1.70)[b]</td><td>0.723
(1.41)</td><td>-0.0004
(-0.84)</td><td>174.0</td></tr>
<tr><td>0.003
(1.69)[b]</td><td>-0.448
(-2.40)[a]</td><td>-0.083
(-1.53)[b]</td><td>-0.185
(-3.47)[a]</td><td>-0.0005
(-2.23)[a]</td><td>-0.00001
(-1.76)[b]</td><td>-0.003
(-0.47)</td><td>143.6</td></tr>
<tr><td>-0.001
(-0.61)</td><td>1.064
(3.17)[a]</td><td>0.156
(2.32)[a]</td><td>-0.320
(-5.04)[a]</td><td>-0.0006
(-2.24)[a]</td><td>-0.0000
(-0.75)</td><td>-0.0002
(-0.31)</td><td>345.4</td></tr>
<tr><td>0.0002
(0.09)</td><td>0.426
(2.33)[a]</td><td>-0.100
(-1.96)[a]</td><td>0.066
(1.75)[b]</td><td>-0.00002
(-0.14)</td><td>0.0000
(-0.09)</td><td>0.0004
(0.68)</td><td>177.0</td></tr>
<tr><td>0.002
(1.07)</td><td>0.156
(0.99)</td><td>0.013
(0.25)</td><td>-0.001
(-0.03)</td><td>-0.0003
(-1.88)[b]</td><td>0.000001
(0.11)</td><td>-0.0003
(-0.75)</td><td>48.7</td></tr>
<tr><td>-0.001
(-0.80)</td><td>0.102
(0.61)</td><td>-0.048
(-0.94)</td><td>0.017
(0.51)</td><td>0.0004
(2.71)[a]</td><td>0.00001
(1.93)[b]</td><td>0.0001
(0.18)</td><td>152.6</td></tr>
<tr><td>0.0005
(0.24)</td><td>-0.203
(-0.93)</td><td>0.090
(1.37)</td><td>-0.070
(-1.79)[b]</td><td>-0.0002
(-1.25)</td><td>0.00000
(0.06)</td><td>0.0003
(0.54)</td><td>58.13</td></tr>
<tr><td>0.0006
(0.33)</td><td>-0.589
(-3.22)[a]</td><td>0.064
(1.28)</td><td>0.011
(0.32)</td><td>-0.0001
(-0.92)</td><td>-0.00001
(-1.78)[b]</td><td>-0.00005
(-0.10)</td><td>158.5</td></tr>
<tr><td>-0.0003
(-0.15)</td><td>0.122
(0.67)</td><td>-0.043
(-0.82)</td><td>0.019
(0.52)</td><td>-0.0002
(-1.11)</td><td>-0.00001
(-0.25)</td><td>0.0003
(0.55)</td><td>211.5</td></tr>
<tr><td>0.00002
(0.01)</td><td>-0.405
(-2.26)[a]</td><td>0.033
(0.65)</td><td>0.033
(0.97)</td><td>-0.0002
(-0.99)</td><td>-0.00001
(-2.45)[a]</td><td>-0.0003
(-0.50)</td><td>177.2</td></tr>
</table>

Table 6.4.   Continued

			Coefficient of			
Votes	Constant	Central City Residents	% Union Members	Consumers	RADA	% Black
Defense spending	2.588 (0.94)	−0.012 (−2.70)[a]	−0.023 (−1.37)	−0.1000 (−1.73)[b]	−0.047 (−7.46)[a]	0.003 (0.31)
Debt limit increase	−0.996 (−0.40)	0.008 (1.99)[a]	0.028 (1.92)[a]	−0.020 (−0.40)	0.005 (1.16)	−0.004 (−0.44)
Civil service annuity	1.860 (0.56)	0.028 (4.46)[a]	0.036 (1.92)[b]	0.093 (1.41)	0.036 (5.37)[a]	0.004 (0.33)
Consumer protection	3.244 (1.04)	−0.019 (−3.39)[a]	−0.094 (−4.80)[a]	0.092 (1.46)	0.056 (7.98)[a]	0.012 (0.96)
Minimum wage increase	4.037 (0.37)	0.022 (2.64)[a]	0.070 (2.53)[a]	−0.199 (−2.12)[a]	0.048 (4.92)[a]	−0.020 (−1.25)
Campaign spending	2.980 (0.60)	0.008 (1.10)	0.023 (0.90)	0.128 (1.43)	0.030 (3.55)[a]	0.025 (1.11)
Rice production	−4.960 (−1.75)[b]	0.003 (0.75)	0.028 (1.81)[b]	−0.093 (−1.71)[b]	−0.007 (−1.36)	−0.013 (−1.29)
Rice production (consider)	−8.042 (−2.77)[a]	0.006 (1.20)	0.050 (2.71)[a]	−0.001 (−0.02)	0.028 (4.58)[a]	−0.0006 (−0.06)
Antihijacking	−5.179 (−1.37)	0.015 (2.99)[a]	0.065 (3.22)[a]	−0.051 (−0.76)	0.071 (8.76)[a]	0.027 (2.49)[a]
Energy	0.322 (0.10)	−0.005 (−1.23)	0.007 (0.39)	−0.247 (−4.04)[a]	−0.027 (−4.72)[a]	−0.012 (−1.10)

Note: t-values in parentheses; maximum-likelihood ratio significant at the 0.01 level for all equations.
[a]Significant at the 0.05 level.
[b]Significant at the 0.10 level.

the bill dealing with increasing the limit for the national debt. This last result was most surprising: Borcherding (1977) and others have argued that much of the impetus for the growth of government has come from government employees; thus, government spending in any given district should be important in influencing the vote of that district's representative on the size of government. Since DOD and HEW are responsible for most government spending, we retested our equation using total government spending in a district; however, it was still insignificant as an influence on voting by

Table 6.4. Continued

			Coefficient of				Likeli-hood
HEW Spending	Education	Age	% Farmers	Oil Production	Coal Production	DOD Spending	Ratio Test
−0.001	0.021	−0.038	−0.006	0.0006	0.00001	0.0001	127.6
(−0.63)	(0.13)	(−0.73)	(−0.18)	(3.65)[a]	(−1.37)	(0.24)	
−0.001	0.060	−0.006	−0.004	0.0002	0.00001	−0.0002	24.76
(−0.63)	(0.43)	(−0.14)	(−0.15)	(1.74)[b]	(1.66)[b]	(−0.43)	
0.001	−0.570	0.080	−0.004	−0.0002	−0.00001	0.001	84.62
(0.48)	(−2.83)[a]	(1.43)	(−0.11)	(−1.33)	(−1.26)	(2.14)[a]	
0.00002	−0.405	0.033	0.033	−0.0002	−0.00001	−0.000	177.2
(0.01)	(−2.26)[a]	(0.65)	(0.97)	(−0.99)	(−2.45)[a]	(−0.49)	
0.004	−0.704	0.124	−0.085	−0.0005	−0.00001	0.0006	71.65
(1.80)[b]	(−2.40)[a]	(1.64)[b]	(−1.88)[b]	(−2.58)[a]	(−1.66)[b]	(0.90)	
0.002	−0.704	0.116	−0.022	−0.0004	−0.00005	0.0007	46.65
(0.85)	(−2.33)[a]	(1.55)	(−0.49)	(−1.99)[a]	(−0.72)	(1.08)	
0.003	0.193	0.031	−0.013	−0.001	−0.00002	0.0006	44.57
(1.80)[b]	(1.14)	(0.68)	(−0.42)	(−3.08)[a]	(−3.22)[a]	(0.12)	
−0.0004	0.419	0.080	−0.010	−0.001	−0.00001	−0.001	131.1
(−0.22)	(2.53)[a]	(1.58)[b]	(−0.29)	(−4.61)[a]	(−1.77)[b]	(−1.73)[b]	
0.0007	0.526	−0.101	0.055	−0.0003	−0.00002	−0.0004	168.5
(0.36)	(2.46)[a]	(−1.71)[b]	(1.50)	(−1.38)	(−2.95)[a]	(−0.72)	
−0.003	0.660	−0.135	0.047	0.0016	0.000005	−0.00052	146.1
(−1.49)	(3.51)[a]	(−2.61)[a]	(1.46)	(5.17)[a]	(0.10)	(−1.07)	

representatives. Our results from this vote and the evidence about the general insignificance of government spending indicate that theories that explain government behavior on the basis of the actions of government employees may not be valid. If these theories are valid, our evidence indicates that some channel other than voting is required to explain the influence of government employees.

The number of blacks in a district was significant only three times; the central city variable may have picked up the influence of blacks as voters (the correlation between these variables was 0.4). The average age of the population over eighteen was significant ten times with no particular pattern; we have no theory about what this variable measures.

Our findings were remarkably robust: If the RADA variable was positive on some vote, the variables of central city residents, consumers, and unions were almost invariably positive. Also, if this coalition favored one aspect of some program, it seemed to favor almost all aspects of the program, as shown by the consistency of votes over the nine issues we identified as "urban" issues.

In summary, our results indicate that a liberal coalition, consistent in its makeup, exists in Congress and that ideology is an important determinant of voting behavior. We have not directly tested for logrolling, but our economic variables seem indirectly to measure members of whatever logrolling coalitions exist in Congress. The significance of the RADA variable when all economic interests are included indicates that it probably measures something other than logrolling; however, in the following section we test more specifically the possibility that "liberalism" is a measure of the extent to which representatives belong to a logrolling coalition.

ANALYSIS OF VOTES: CONDITIONAL PROBABILITY MODEL

ADA ratings are claimed to be a measure of ideology. However, an alternative explanation is that ADA ratings may be a measure of logrolling, by which we mean something more than simple vote trading. A form of implicit logrolling may occur if, for example, representatives from union districts agree to vote in favor of bills that transfer funds to central cities whenever such bills occur, provided that representatives from central cities agree to vote in favor of union bills whenever such bills occur. If ADA ratings do, in fact, measure logrolling, being a liberal would simply mean being a member of the coalition of economic interests that includes people interested in consumer issues, residents of central cities, and union members; being a conservative would mean being a member of the coalition of farmers and oil producers. If these definitions of liberal and conservative are correct, voting has no ideological component (where ideology is defined as non-self-interested voting); rather, all voting must be based either on direct self-interest or on logrolling.

To test whether ADA ratings measure logrolling, we have used a set of twelve bills chosen to eliminate issues that appeal to the same economic interests. For each bill, conditional logit estimates were derived by treating all but one of the jointly dependent dichotomous variables as if they were explanatory exogenous variables. Since certain endogenous variables or levels of these variables are held fixed in the conditional probability model (and therefore treated as exogenous), estimators based on this model will not be the same as those obtained from the unconstrained model. In the context of logistic models, the conditional probability function corresponds to the structural equation of the stimultaneous equations approach to the analysis of continuously variable, jointly dependent, endogenous variables. Although this method is known to be inappropriate in the case of continuously variable data, it is commonly used with qualitative data. An alternative would be to obtain full-information estimators from an unconstrained model. However, existing programs using this technique are unable to handle more than four endogenous variables, too few to test the logrolling hypothesis (Nerlove and Press 1973).

Table 6.5 presents estimates of the conditional probability functions for each of the dependent variables as functions of the exogenous variables and the remaining eleven endogenous variables. The coefficients of the exogenous variables show a remarkable degree of stability relative to the logit model. In some cases the exogenous coefficients are insignificant. Unions become insignificant in the minimum wage vote; coal production is insignificant in the mining bill; consumer interest is insignificant in the consumer protection bill. In conditional probability models the included endogenous (treated as exogenous) variables have a tendency to reduce the significance level of the exogenous variables. The relatively few changes suggest that the logit model is a reliable indicator of the existence of coalitions and of the influence of ideology.

The conditional probability model provides evidence for the existence of coalitions insofar as many of the votes are associated significantly with each other.[3] The coalitions that appear through the voting analysis seem to be the same as the coalitions identified earlier. In addition, the ideological variable RADA is significant in eight of the twelve votes. Three of the twelve votes — busing, death penalty for airline hijackers, and consumer protection — would seem to be almost pure ideological votes, and RADA is significant in these votes, but it is also significant in votes dealing with the highway program, surface mining, housing, and defense spending, which are primarily economic. RADA is also significant in the vote dealing with campaign financing, which may be ideological but may also be economic insofar as it will influence the effective political power of various groups. In any event, while ADA may serve in part to monitor membership in a

Table 6.5. Conditional Estimates of the Univariate Conditional
Logit Parameters for Congressional Votes, 1974

Variables	Planning Grants	Highway Program	Campaign Spending Act	Surface Mining	Housing Subsidies
			Dependent Variables: Votes, 1974		
Constant	3.977	−23.614	9.477	0.937	−6.940
	(1.16)	(−3.72)[a]	(1.52)	(0.27)	(−2.11)[a]
Central	0.015	0.031	−0.017	0.004	0.011
city residents	(2.71)[a]	(3.70)[a]	(−1.60)	(0.68)	(2.10)[a]
% union	0.0002	0.068	−0.070	0.031	−0.005
members	(0.01)	(2.41)[a]	(−2.03)[a]	(1.31)	(−0.26)
Consumers	0.078	0.395	0.018	−0.073	0.292
	(1.15)	(3.74)[a]	(0.14)	(−0.92)	(4.08)[a]
RADA	0.004	0.055	−0.030	−0.021	0.042
	(0.49)	(4.48)[a]	(−1.84)[b]	(−2.25)[a]	(5.14)[a]
% black	0.020	0.023	0.0003	−0.002	0.021
	(1.60)	(1.21)	(0.01)	(−0.14)	(1.80)[b]
HEW spending	−0.001	−0.003	0.003	−0.001	0.003
	(−0.80)	(−1.13)	(0.84)	(−0.55)	(1.39)
Education	−0.465	1.147	−0.476	−0.058	0.294
	(−2.41)[a]	(3.06)[a]	(−1.31)	(−0.31)	(1.66)[b]
Age	−0.019	0.142	−0.028	0.0001	0.015
	(−0.35)	(1.89)[b]	(−0.31)	(0.00)	(0.27)
% farmers	−0.085	−0.367	0.037	0.018	−0.010
	(−2.06)[b]	(−4.98)[a]	(0.36)	(0.43)	(−0.27)
Oil production	−0.0003	−0.0004	−0.0002	0.0004	−0.0004
	(−1.65)[b]	(−1.39)	(−0.79)	(1.77)[b]	(−2.44)[a]
Coal	−0.00002	0.000002	0.000008	0.000004	−0.000002
production	(−3.08)[a]	(0.27)	(0.78)	(0.77)	(−0.36)
DOD/P	−0.0012	0.000004	0.0009	−0.00004	−0.0006
	(−2.23)[a]	(0.01)	(1.17)	(−0.06)	(−1.24)
Planning	—	0.613	0.771	0.159	0.360
grants		(1.60)	(1.34)	(0.47)	(1.17)
Highway	0.920	—	1.634	−1.205	−0.913
program	(2.50)[a]		(2.50)[a]	(−2.95)[a]	(−2.35)[a]
Campaign	0.671	1.263	—	0.113	−0.028
spending act	(1.24)	(1.93)[b]		(0.23)	(0.06)
Surface	0.335	−1.161	0.446	—	0.194
mining	(0.97)	(−2.59)[a]	(0.82)		(0.58)
Housing	0.333	−1.810	0.198	−0.0047	—
subsidies	(1.11)	(−1.88)[b]	(0.36)	(−0.01)	
Civil service	0.634	0.028	0.173	−0.447	1.013
annuity	(1.93)[b]	(0.06)	(0.39)	(−1.26)	(3.10)[a]
Public	1.191	−0.695	1.743	−1.250	0.059
jobs	(3.30)[a]	(−1.37)	(2.32)[a]	(−3.42)[a]	(0.16)
Defense	0.317	−1.100	−0.807	0.684	0.182
spending	(1.02)	(−2.81)[a]	(−1.68)[b]	(2.25)[a]	(0.62)
Consumer	−0.216	0.364	−2.094	0.716	0.563
protection	(−0.59)	(0.71)	(−2.80)[a]	(2.00)[a]	(1.51)
Minimum	0.293	0.305	1.695	−1.589	−0.895
wage	(0.54)	(0.44)	(3.41)[a]	(−2.61)[a]	(−1.83)[b]

Table 6.5   Continued

		Dependent Variables: Votes, 1974				
Civil Service Annuity	Public Jobs	Defense Spending	Consumer Protection	Minimum Wage	Prohibit Busing	Anti-hijacking
2.659	0.554	1.283	6.963	5.528	2.958	-5.859
(0.71)	(0.13)	(0.42)	(1.78)[b]	(0.84)	(0.61)	(-1.37)
0.018	0.018	-0.0054	0.00015	0.014	-0.023	0.005
(2.46)[a]	(2.40)[a]	(-1.03)	(0.02)	(1.22)	(-3.66)[a]	(0.93)
-0.002	0.081	0.009	-0.052	0.046	-0.049	0.033
(-0.07)	(3.11)[a]	(0.46)	(-2.12)[a]	(1.18)	(-1.94)[b]	(1.48)
0.022	-0.101	-0.037	-0.137	-0.363	-0.173	-0.091
(0.27)	(-1.04)	(-0.55)	(-1.46)	(-2.64)[a]	(-2.03)[a]	(-1.16)
0.001	0.015	-0.030	-0.024	0.014	-0.038	0.057
(0.11)	(1.32)	(-3.63)[a]	(-2.33)[a]	(0.83)	(-3.56)[a]	(5.30)[a]
-0.006	0.0015	0.007	-0.018	-0.045	-0.011	0.031
(-0.45)	(0.10)	(0.71)	(-1.13)	(-2.14)[a]	(-0.74)	(2.56)[a]
-0.0009	-0.002	-0.0015	-0.002	0.033	0.0004	0.001
(-0.41)	(-0.96)	(-0.85)	(-0.68)	(1.06)	(0.16)	(0.65)
-0.464	-0.076	-0.046	0.240	-0.337	-0.296	0.615
(-2.08)[a]	(-0.32)	(-0.27)	(1.07)	(-0.92)	(-1.18)	(2.63)[a]
0.037	-0.040	0.008	-0.094	0.063	0.153	-0.076
(0.60)	(-0.58)	(0.15)	(-1.47)	(0.64)	(2.14)[a]	(-1.20)
0.025	0.073	-0.033	0.059	-0.098	-0.172	0.017
(0.58)	(1.45)	(-0.86)	(1.42)	(-1.42)	(-3.66)[a]	(0.36)
0.0001	0.00012	0.0006	-0.0003	-0.0004	-0.00002	-0.0004
(0.53)	(0.54)	(3.28)[a]	(-1.44)	(-1.57)	(-0.08)	(-1.60)
0.0000002	-0.00001	0.00001	0.0000001	-0.000003	-0.000006	-0.00002
(0.04)	(-1.12)	(1.97)[a]	(0.02)	(-0.24)	(-0.96)	(-2.80)[a]
0.0015	-0.0002	0.00009	-0.0005	-0.000007	0.0006	-0.0004
(2.58)[a]	(-0.30)	(0.18)	(-0.67)	(-0.09)	(0.92)	(-0.68)
0.721	1.343	0.263	-0.207	0.362	-0.350	-0.261
(2.08)[a]	(3.60)[a]	(0.86)	(-0.56)	(0.60)	(-0.91)	(-0.72)
0.003	-0.338	-0.969	-0.101	-0.043	-0.275	0.079
(0.01)[a]	(-0.72)	(-2.68)[a]	(-0.22)	(-0.58)	(-0.57)	(0.17)
0.240	1.661	-0.638	-1.759	1.761	-0.949	-0.839
(0.57)	(2.19)[a]	(-1.38)	(-2.44)[a]	(3.39)[a]	(-0.99)	(-1.32)
-0.532	-1.273	0.565	0.705	-1.424	1.203	0.209
(-1.50)	(-3.41)[a]	(1.85)[b]	(1.89)[b]	(-2.22)[a]	(2.33)[a]	(0.46)
1.074	0.152	0.119	0.478	-1.018	0.893	-0.519
(3.17)[a]	(0.39)	(0.41)	(1.25)	(-1.65)[b]	(2.41)[a]	(-1.43)
—	0.608	0.142	-1.015	0.961	-0.036	0.314
	(1.53)	(0.42)	(-2.52)[a]	(1.83)[b]	(-0.06)	(1.68)[b]
0.683	—	-1.232	-1.847	1.071	0.142	0.686
(1.74)[b]		(-3.59)[a]	(-4.95)[a]	(1.24)	(0.26)	(1.42)
-0.031	-1.177	—	0.096	-0.290	-0.472	0.451
(-0.09)	(-3.35)[a]		(0.26)	(-0.56)	(-1.10)	(1.12)
-1.093	-1.894	0.111	—	-1.181	0.797	-0.177
(-2.78)[a]	(-4.99)[a]	(0.32)		(-1.45)	(1.42)	(-0.37)
1.015	0.581	0.125	-0.978	—	-0.072	0.934
(2.35)[a]	(0.76)	(0.26)	(-1.30)		(-0.06)	(1.08)

Table 6.5.   Continued

	Dependent Variables: Votes, 1974				
Variables	Planning Grants	Highway Program	Campaign Spending Act	Surface Mining	Housing Subsidies
Prohibit	−0.627	−0.432	−1.146	1.205	0.986
busing	(−1.77)[b]	(−0.82)	(−1.21)	(2.46)[a]	(2.69)[a]
Antihijacking	−0.028	0.431	−0.398	−0.024	−0.402
	(−0.08)	(0.90)	(−0.61)	(−0.06)	(−1.15)
Likelihood ratio test	199.1	380.3	135.7	255.0	86.0

Note: t-values in parentheses; maximum-likelihood ratio significant at the 0.01 level for all equations.
[a]Significant at the 0.05 level.
[b]Significant at the 0.10 level.

logrolling coalition, this variable clearly measures other things as well. We have been unable to reject the hypothesis that ideology is important in explaining the voting behavior of congressional representatives.

When we began our research on voting by congressional representatives, we were convinced that Stigler's (1971) hypothesis was correct. That is, we were convinced that voting could be explained entirely on the basis of economic interests and that ideology would not be significant if all relevant economic variables were controlled. In this chapter we have attempted to adjust for all economic variables in two ways: by controlling for economic variables in each vote and by examining votes as a function of each other to test for logrolling. Nevertheless, we have found that ideology is significant in explaining voting by representatives on bills with primarily economic components. Thus, we cannot continue to argue that ideology is insignificant in explaining voting behavior; something significantly and systematically associated with voting appears to correlate with the ratings given to members of Congress by ideological groups. Whether this "something" is ideology or whether it is some economic interest that we have been unable to measure must remain an open question.

This research can be extended in several directions. First, we have used as economic interests the characteristics of constituents. However, Silberman and Durden (1976), in their study of minimum wages, used campaign contributions by various interest groups as their measure of economic interest. In later chapters we will extend our results to include contributions.

Second, as we have seen, economists do not have a well-developed theory of the nature of ideology. Schumpeter (1950) argues that people who have an

Table 6.5.   Continued

			Dependent Variables: Votes, 1974			
Civil Service Annuity	Public Jobs	Defense Spending	Consumer Protection	Minimum Wage	Prohibit Busing	Anti- hijacking
−0.037	0.047	−0.222	0.692	−0.180	—	−1.582
(−0.07)	(0.09)	(−0.59)	(1.26)	(−0.15)		(−4.56)[a]
0.846	0.464	0.144	−0.414	1.283	−1.618	—
(1.76)[b]	(0.95)	(0.39)	(−0.839)	(1.29)	(−4.67)[a]	
159.2	329.1	177.9	320.57	154.1	232.5	208.5

interest in strong government are able to convince others that government control is desirable; to the extent that this theory is correct, it requires further development and expansion. (The results of our analysis indicate that Schumpeter's theory may well be correct.) Psychologists may have a comparative advantage in developing theories of ideology, but the issue has sufficient implications for economic policy making to induce economists not to rely solely on psychological research. The results presented in this chapter indicate a weakness of economics as a positive science insofar as legislation cannot be fully explained on the basis of economic factors. But the results also indicate a strength of normative economics: If we economists can convince others of the correctness of our ideas, we may be able to influence their behavior.

Like others who have written on topics related to public policy, we end with a policy prescription — but our suggestion is based on empirical evidence that seems to indicate that such suggestions may, in fact, matter.

NOTES

1. Northern Democrats are sometimes thought of as liberals, and Republicans and southern Democrats as conservatives. We have examined the relation between party and region in the ADA ratings, as shown on p. 53. These variables explain some, but not all, of the ratings.

2. Data sources: data on income, central city residents, blacks, education, age, DOD, and HEW from the *Almanac of American Politics* (1974); data on union membership from U.S. Department of Labor (1975); data on oil production from the American Petroleum Institute (1975); data on coal production from U.S. Bureau of Mines (1975). Number of subscribers by

state to *Consumer Reports* was obtained from Consumers' Union. Interest group ratings and roll call votes are from the *Congressional Quarterly Almanac* (1974).

3. The conditional probability model may have problems with multicollinearity since some of the votes are correlated. The votes were selected to reduce this effect, and, in general, the correlations were quite low.

7 EMPIRICAL ESTIMATION OF THE GENERAL EQUILIBRIUM MODEL

In the last several chapters we have examined various measures of ideology, such as membership in public interest lobbies and ADA ratings earned by members of Congress, and have found that each of these measures seems to be associated with voting. The model of congressional voting developed in chapter 4 is more general than any of the models we have so far investigated; it shows a simultaneous relationship between voting by representatives on bills, voting by constituents in congressional elections, and contributions to representatives. The relationship is simultaneous in the sense that each of these factors influences the others. In this chapter we empirically test this model.

DATA AND EMPIRICAL SPECIFICATION

Data

Votes. As our sample we have used voting in 1979 on eight bills, chosen because they represent a set of issues with relatively broad economic impact. The bills are as follows:

1. Public Debt Limit: bill to increase the public debt limit from $798 billion to $830 billion (passed, 212-195);
2. Wage-Price Council Reauthorization: bill to reauthorize the Wage-Price Council through 30 September 1980 and increase its appropriation (passed, 242-175);
3. Independent Agencies Appropriation: amendment to increase Environmental Protection Agency funds by $4 million for groundwater contamination research and by $6 million for research into methods for controlling hazardous substances (rejected, 129-237);
4. Labor Appropriations: amendment to reduce OSHA appropriations by $10.3 million (rejected, 177-240);
5. Windfall Profits Tax: bill to provide a tax rate of 70 percent and a permanent tax on oil price increases (adjusted for inflation plus 2 percent annually) of more than seventeen dollars per barrel (passed, 230-185);
6. Federal Trade Commission Authorization: amendment to prohibit the FTC from prosecuting antitrust cases against agricultural coops or from investigating agricultural marketing orders (passed, 245-139);
7. Hospital Cost Control: substitute amendment to establish a three-year study commission on hospital costs (passed, 234-166);
8. HEW Appropriations: amendment to reduce HEW appropriation by $500 million, the reduction to be taken from programs containing waste, fraud, and abuse (passed, 263-152).

Econometric techniques were greatly simplified by having the same number of votes on each bill; therefore, we assigned votes to each nonvoting representative on the basis of the votes of the majority of other representatives from the same state. Where a tie made such assignment impossible, a random process was used.

In some cases (e.g., the windfall profits tax or hospital cost control) well-defined interest groups were involved with the issue in question; in other cases (e.g., wage-price controls or the debt limit) it was less clear who might favor or oppose a bill. Many of these bills are relevant to our attempt to ascertain the source of the regulatory legislation that has been passed in the last several years.

Contributions. The Federal Election Commission has gathered data on contributions from various sources of congressional campaigns for 1978. We have aggregated these data into six categories: *Individual contributions* include contributions from $101-$499 and contributions of over $500.

Under *major party contributions* we include expenditures on behalf of candidates by political parties. *Business contributions* include corporate contributions and contributions from corporations without stock. *Union contributions* are from labor organizations; *cooperative contributions* are primarily those of dairy cooperatives and of savings and loan associations. The final category is *medical contributions* — that is, contributions from donors in health-related fields. In all cases contributions include both direct contributions and in kind contributions of goods, services, or property. The amount contributed by each type of organization to the campaigns of victorious candidates is reported in table 7.1. In some of the equations that follow, we use contributions from each type of group; in other equations we are concerned with the total received by the candidate. We also use contributions received by the losing candidate (always used in an aggregate form).

Characteristics of Constituents and Representatives. We have used data on constituent characteristics in several categories.[1] The following data are based on congressional district, the preferred form: central city residents, education, defense spending, HEW spending, other government spending per capita, age, percentage of farmers, percentage of blacks, and percentage of voters for Gerald Ford in the 1978 presidential election. The following data are statewide since these variables were not available by district: union membership, oil production, coal production, and membership in Consumers' Union.

In addition to the data on constituents, we have also used data on the seniority, electoral margin, and party of each representative.

Ideology. Our basic measures of ideology are (1) the percentage of voters in the representative's district who voted for Gerald Ford in the 1978 presiden-

Table 7.1. Political Contributions to Victorious Candidates, 1978

Category	Amount
Individual	$13,855,000
Party	3,297,838
Business	5,363,320
Labor	4,760,007
Cooperative	549,953
Medical	6,296,080

Source: Data from Federal Election Commission (1979).

tial election and (2) the ADA rating earned by the representative. Obviously, part of the reason for choosing between Ford or Carter was economic. However, we have controlled for most of the important economic variables in the district — central city residence, race, and education (highly correlated with income and occupation) — and thus we argue that the Ford variable may be a measure of ideology independent of economic interest. In previous research the ADA ratings earned by representatives have been interpreted as measures of ideology and have been found significant in explaining voting. Here we measure both constituents' ideology and the representative's ideology. While we claim that the Ford-Carter vote and the ADA rating are measures of ideology, they may be measures of some economic characteristic we have been unable to specify. In any event, it seems important to control for ideology in determining the effect of specifically economic factors on congressional voting.

Econometric Techniques

As we have seen, a large number of studies have attempted to quantify the impact of voting determinants on voting. Empirically, cross-sectional data of voting patterns of representatives have dominated. All of the analyses have been partial equilibrium in technique; these studies have found a significant relationship between economic and ideological variables and voting. This chapter adds two potentially important variables to the study of determinants of voting: the electoral margin and the contributions received by representative and opponent. These additional variables suggest that the unilateral partial equilibrium approach common to all other studies of voting may be inappropriate — a potentially serious matter since the voting of a representative may clearly affect contributions and electoral margins as well as be affected by them.

From a formal point of view this would imply that voting is simultaneously determined with contributions and electoral margins. Thus, a mixed logit model following the principles of Schmidt and Strauss (1975, 1976) and Nerlove and Press (1973) is used. The three equations are

$$\bar{V} = \alpha(M, \bar{F}, \bar{I}, \bar{S}), \tag{7.1}$$

$$\bar{F} = \beta\,(\bar{V}, \bar{S}, TL), \tag{7.2}$$

$$M = \gamma\,(\bar{V}, \bar{I}, \bar{S}, TF, TL). \tag{7.3}$$

This set of simultaneous equations provides the structural relationship necessary for quantifying the separate effects of the determinants of voting, electoral margins, and contributions.

EMPIRICAL RESULTS

The results of the second stage of two-stage simultaneous estimation procedure with votes, contributions, and margin as endogenous variables are reported in tables 7.2, 7.3, and 7.4. The first-stage results of endogenous variables as a function of all the exogenous variables are not reported. The predicted value of votes, margin, and contributions from the first stage are used in the appropriate equations. Table 7.2 is the heart of our analysis. It indicates which interest groups, measured both in terms of membership in a representative's district and in terms of contributions to campaigns, favor various types of legislation. We will analyze particular votes and interest groups later. Here we merely indicate that the results of the first-stage estimation, measured in terms of R^2 and also of percentage of votes predicted correctly, are reasonably good.[2] All coefficients in tables 7.2, 7.3, and 7.4 are point elasticities evaluated at the mean.[3]

In table 7.3 we examine the factors associated with contributions from the various types of contributors. The independent variables in these equations are party (Democrat = 1), seniority, contributions received by the loser, a dummy that takes the value of 1 if the winner was in a primary, and an index of voting by the representative on the eight issues. This index was constructed as a measure of the percentage of time the representative voted "conservatively." A representative who voted all eight times as the Ford vote would predict would receive a +1 score on this index, and a representative who voted against the Ford vote would receive a −1. We find in several cases that party is significant (individuals, unions, and cooperatives give to Democrats and businesses give to Republicans). The negative sign on party in the party contribution equation indicates that the Republican party contributes more than the Democratic party.

We find in five cases that total contributions received by the loser in the election are significant and positive in explaining contributions received by the winner. This result is consistent with the result of Jacobson (1980), who argued that incumbents are able to receive as much money as they desire and that they desire more money when they are in close elections against strong opponents. A measure of the strength of the opponent is the amount of contributions the opponent is able to obtain. As we shall see, our results on the effect of contributions on electoral margin are also consistent with Jacobson's argument. It is interesting that his results, which were found in a single equation model explaining contributions, carry through into our model, which is a simultaneous equation model. Primary is significant five times and has a positive sign in four cases where significant; thus, business, individuals, parties, and medical contributors give more to candidates who are

Table 7.2. Congressional Votes (General Issues), 1978

Variables	Debt Limit	Wage-Price Controls	EPA Funds	OSHA Appropriations	Windfall Profits	FTC Authorization	Hospital Cost Control	HEW Appropriations
Constant term	-5.673 (-1.73)[a]	0.999 (0.04)	2.865 (1.94)[a]	0.548 (0.18)	-2.312 (-0.55)	2.098 (0.94)	4.805 (0.56)	-11.340 (2.75)[a]
Seniority	0.293 (3.11)[a]	0.056 (0.75)	-0.180 (-1.53)[a]	0.160 (2.00)[a]	0.255 (1.65)[a]	0.325 (3.35)[a]	-0.019 (-0.10)	0.335 (2.86)[a]
% union members	0.052 (0.23)	-0.046 (-0.22)	0.904 (3.04)[a]	0.882 (3.75)[a]	0.068 (0.24)	0.224 (0.93)	0.430 (0.89)	0.800 (2.40)[a]
Ford vote	-0.643 (-1.32)[a]	-0.816 (-1.99)[a]	-0.493 (-0.88)	-0.596 (-1.34)[a]	-1.109 (-1.93)[a]	-0.734 (-1.49)[a]	-1.515 (-1.78)[a]	-0.491 (-0.72)
ADA	0.385 (1.53)[a]	0.167 (0.84)	0.579 (1.78)[a]	0.830 (3.32)[a]	0.391 (1.09)	0.853 (3.29)[a]	1.120 (1.81)[a]	1.936 (4.90)[a]
Electoral margin	3.217 (2.10)[a]	0.433 (0.35)	-3.995 (-2.47)[a]	0.085 (0.07)	2.676 (1.01)	-2.040 (-1.50)[a]	-2.380 (-0.69)	5.841 (2.89)[a]
Labor contributions	0.813 (3.71)[a]	0.523 (3.07)[a]	-0.839 (-3.22)[a]	0.160 (1.02)	0.968 (4.12)[a]	-0.317 (-1.32)[a]	-0.106 (-0.33)	0.498 (1.61)[a]
Business contributions	0.285 (0.59)	-0.017 (-0.45)	-0.459 (-0.87)	0.027 (0.07)	-0.264 (-0.41)	-0.784 (-1.90)[a]	-0.298 (-0.36)	0.080 (0.10)
Individual contributions	0.141 (0.76)	-0.214 (-1.33)[a]	0.739 (3.38)[a]	0.131 (0.93)	—	0.249 (1.02)	0.163 (0.56)	0.129 (0.49)
Cooperative contributions	—	—	0.058 (0.55)	—	—	-0.043 (-0.19)	—	—
Medical contributions	—	—	-1.161 (-1.32)[a]	-0.240 (-0.38)	—	—	-1.341 (-0.80)	1.564 (2.07)[a]

Age	1.075 (0.93)	—	—	—	—	—	—	0.029 (0.02)
Central city residents	0.131 (1.44)[a]	0.048 (0.62)	—	—	0.0099 (0.08)	—	0.143 (0.82)	-0.100 (-0.98)
Federal spending	0.023 (0.11)	—	—	—	—	—	—	—
Education	—	0.125 (0.12)	-3.688 (-1.87)[a]	-1.963 (-1.44)[a]	—	—	-1.741 (-0.51)	—
% black	—	-0.0045 (-0.65)	—	-0.020 (-0.30)	-0.270 (-2.67)[a]	—	—	-0.061 (-0.61)
HEW spending	—	-0.049 (-0.19)	—	0.380 (1.63)[a]	—	—	0.167 (0.39)	0.303 (0.83)
% farmers	—	-0.096 (-1.80)[a]	—	—	—	-0.312 (-1.64)[a]	—	—
Consumers	—	0.031 (1.07)	0.032 (0.79)	-0.035 (-1.39)[a]	—	0.037 (1.15)	0.055 (1.05)	—
Defense spending	—	—	—	—	-0.017 (-0.19)	—	—	—
Coal production	—	—	—	—	-0.088 (-1.79)[a]	—	—	—
Oil production	—	—	—	—	-0.178 (-1.90)[a]	—	—	—
R^2	0.39	0.35	0.17	0.60	0.66	0.54	0.61	0.53
% correct forecast	0.81	0.81	0.72	0.88	0.92	0.88	0.92	0.87

Note: Coefficients are mean point elasticities.
[a] t-values significant at the 0.10 level.

Table 7.3. Determinants of Contributions (General Issues), 1978

Category of Contribution	Constant Term	Party	Total Loser Contributions	Dummy Primary	Seniority	Vote Index	R^2
Business	0.812	−0.115	0.136	0.087	0.041	0.039	0.31
	$(7.26)^a$	$(−1.54)^a$	$(5.17)^a$	$(3.73)^a$	(0.76)	$(6.96)^a$	
Individual	0.601	0.213	0.252	0.090	−0.180	0.228	0.26
	$(4.47)^a$	$(2.36)^a$	$(7.96)^a$	$(3.19)^a$	$(−2.80)^a$	$(3.40)^a$	
Union	0.700	0.232	0.293	−0.050	−0.113	−0.639	0.43
	$(4.79)^a$	$(2.37)^a$	$(8.50)^a$	$(−1.63)^a$	$(−1.60)^a$	$(−8.79)^a$	
Party	1.908	−1.044	0.273	0.099	−0.230		0.60
	$(20.81)^a$	$(−12.56)^a$	$(10.40)^a$	$(4.27)^a$	$(−4.31)^a$		
Medical	0.751	0.061	0.094	0.052	−0.001	0.420	0.29
	$(7.73)^a$	(0.94)	$(4.09)^a$	$(2.55)^a$	(−0.01)	$(8.68)^a$	
Cooperative	0.144	1.073	−0.0028	−0.036	−0.250	0.681	0.10
	(0.56)	$(6.23)^a$	(−0.05)	(−0.36)	$(−2.04)^a$	$(5.31)^a$	

Note: Coefficients are mean point elasticities.
[a] t-values significant at the 0.05 level.

Table 7.4. Determinants of Electoral
Margin (General Issues), 1978

Variables	Margin
Constant term	1.080
	(50.60)[b]
Incumbent	−0.0013
	(−0.59)
Loser's total contributions	−0.61
	(−9.93)[b]
Winner's total contributions	−0.038
	(−2.83)[b]
Seniority	−0.0089
	(−0.80)
Defense spending (VI)[a]	0.0012
	(1.29)
Coal production (VI)	0.00005
	(−0.07)
Age (VI)	(−0.0004)
	(−0.053)
Ford vote (VI)	−0.014
	(−2.75)[b]
% black (VI)	−0.0023
	(−1.76)[b]
Consumers (VI)	0.0024
	(2.60)[b]
% union members (VI)	0.015
	(3.31)[b]
Education (VI)	−0.00003
	(−0.11)
HEW spending (VI)	0.0043
	(1.60)[b]
Federal spending (VI)	−0.0046
	(−1.82)[b]
% farmers (VI)	−0.0039
	(0.96)
Oil production (VI)	0.0011
	(−0.77)
Central city residents (VI)	0.0082
	(2.25)[b]
R^2	0.41

Note: Coefficients are point elasticities at the mean.
  [a]VI = Vote Index; for example, AGE (VI)
= (AGE − $\overline{\text{AGE}}$) · VI.
  [b]t-values significant at the 0.10 level.

facing primary tests. The seniority variable is significant four times and negative where significant — a somewhat surprising result indicating that more senior candidates receive less in contributions. This result may be an indication that candidates with more seniority are less likely to face strong opponents, so that the loser contributions variable adjusts for seniority. The vote index is significant five times. It indicates that businesses, individuals, medical contributors, and cooperatives give to candidates who vote conservatively, while unions give to candidates with liberal voting records. Since party contributions are the sum of Democratic and Republican contributions, and since we are controlling for party in this equation, we have not included the vote index in determining party contributions.

In table 7.4 we examine the determinants of the electoral margin received by the representative. We find that contributions received by both the winner and the loser are significant and negative in explaining margin. Not surprisingly, contributions received by the loser are negative, but at first it might seem that contributions received by the winner should be positively associated with the number of votes the winner would obtain. The result, however, is consistent with Jacobson's (1980) work. If the loser is a strong contender, the winner must solicit funds to counter the challenge, but the winner is not able to completely counter the strength of the loser. Thus, those winners who face strong challengers spend more money but nonetheless do not fare as well. Jacobson also found that money spent by the victor was negatively associated with the vote that the winner received. This result may be somewhat of an artifact in that we had no independent measure of the closeness of the election *before* campaigning began. Jacobson gets the same result, probably for the same reason.

The theory would imply that electoral margin would be a function of the way in which the representative votes as influenced by the characteristics of his or her constituents. In order to test this hypothesis, we have included several interaction terms. These terms were constructed by taking, for several of the $\bar{I}$ variables (the variables measuring characteristics of constituents), the actual level of the variable in each district and subtracting the mean value of the variable across districts. Thus, for example, $U - \bar{U}$ is a measure of unionization in the representative's state relative to the average. Next, we multiplied this value by the predicted value of the vote index (called VI; this index measures the percentage of times the representative voted conservatively).[4] The theory would indicate that, for example, if representatives from more conservative districts (as measured by the Ford vote in the district) voted more conservatively, they should have larger electoral margins. We find this variable significant seven times. Conservative voting was associated with higher electoral margins for representatives from conservative districts, from districts with relatively many blacks, and from districts with relatively large amounts of total federal spending. Conservative voting by representatives was associated with lower margins for representatives from states with relatively many members of Consumers' Union, from states with relatively many union members, from districts with relatively large spending by HEW, and from districts with relatively many central city residents.

RELATIONS BETWEEN LAWS AND INTEREST GROUPS

One of the purposes behind this research is to determine which interest groups favor which laws. In recent years economists have hypothesized that regulatory laws are generally passed to benefit special-interest groups (see Stigler 1971, Peltzman 1976, Rubin 1975, and Posner 1974). This theory seems to have substantial power in explaining the "old-style" regulation; most economists agree that the ICC primarily benefits railroads and trucks and that the CAB primarily benefits airlines. However, more recently passed regulation (e.g., OSHA, the Consumer Protection Agency, some environmental laws, and perhaps some energy regulation) has no obvious beneficiaries. Moreover, wage and price controls are generally a puzzle to economists since the standard economic argument is that such laws generally have little effect on inflation and act mostly as deadweight that results in economic losses. Several of the votes included for study deal with this type of regulation.

The theory developed in chapter 3 indicates which type of variables (constituent characteristics, contributions, votes, margin, seniority) belongs in each equation. It does not tell which of the constituent characteristics should be influential in each vote. In the estimations reported in table 7.2, we have selected, on the basis of past research and intuition, variables that we feel might affect each vote. The number of variables available for inclusion was limited by the identifiability restrictions. Thus, the results are subject to some a priori restrictions on the variables. Nonetheless, we are able to obtain some information from the coefficients on the variables included in explaining these votes.

First, the strongest result, which is consistent with earlier research, is the significance of the ideological variables. In all cases, at least one of these variables is significant, and in many cases both are significant. Both ADA ratings and Ford voting are significant six out of eight times and always have the opposite sign — an indication that both constituent ideology and the ideology of the representative are significant in explaining many of the representative's votes. These findings are consistent with the earlier results showing that measures of ideology are generally significant.

The second important result is that unions generally seem to favor increased government intervention. Union membership is significant three times, and in all cases its sign disagrees with Ford. Union contributions are significant six times and have the opposite sign from Ford in four cases. Thus, unions seem to support increased government intervention, both in cases where unions have a direct interest in such intervention and in cases where the district interest of unions is less obvious (e.g., HEW spending, the windfall profits tax, and the debt limit).

Business contributions are significant only once and agree with Ford, which indicates that these contributions influence recipients toward conservatism. Since most of the bills under study deal with regulation of business, we might have expected business contributors to be more active in opposing government regulation than appears to be the case. Business contributors have an effect on weakening the FTC but have no effect on, for example, OSHA. Contributions for medical groups are not significant in reducing support for the bill to control hospital costs. They do reduce support for the EPA and increase support for HEW. None of the other contributions variables was significant in influencing votes on the bills chosen.

We find that the number of residents in central cities is significant in one case and disagrees with the results of the Ford vote, which indicates that central city residents are in favor of increased government size. Federal spending in the representative's district is not significant in explaining voting on the debt limit, a measure of the size of government. HEW spending is significant in one of the bills, the EPA bill. It is not significant in the bill that affected HEW spending. This result is consistent with the earlier finding that federal spending is generally not significant in explaining congressional voting. Percentage of farmers in the district is significant in explaining voting against the bill that would have increased the power of the FTC over agricultural cooperatives and also in the wage-price control bill. The number of blacks in the district is significant once, and reduces support for the windfall profits tax; members of Consumers Union reduce support for OSHA. Finally, coal and oil production are significant in explaining voting against the windfall profits tax.

VOTING ON URBAN BILLS

The model discussed so far has been a model of voting on issues of general impact. We have also estimated a similar system of equations with nine bills of specific interest to cities. We have performed this reestimation partly because, like all other aspects of the economy, the structure and functioning of cities is becoming increasingly politicized, and we were interested in examining the determinants of this increasing politicization. Local legislation, such as zoning, has always affected cities, but in recent years federal legislation of all sorts has had an increasing impact upon cities. An additional reason for estimating the determinants of voting on urban legislation is to determine the stability of our results. By choosing an additional set of votes, we are able to determine whether our results are caused by the particular set of bills chosen or whether they are more robust. The nature of the estimation process is such that we must reestimate the entire system of equations; we cannot simply examine the determinants of voting on the urban issues by using the parameters of the earlier estimation technique. Thus, tables 7.5, 7.6, and 7.7 are similar to tables 7.2, 7.3, and 7.4 in that they are the outcome of a simultaneous estimation procedure.

We have examined nine bills with some impact upon cities. The bills are as follows:

1. New York City Aid: bill providing federal loan guarantees for $2 billion for fifteen years for New York City bonds (passed, 247–155);
2. HUD-Independent Agencies Appropriations: Brown amendment to reduce appropriations for the Environmental Protection Agency by $133 million (rejected, 173–211);
3. Chrysler Loan Guarantees: bill to authorize $1.5 billion in loan guarantees for Chrysler, to be matched by aid from various other sources (passed, 271–136);
4. HUD-Independent Agencies Appropriations: Nelson amendment to cut $685 million in general revenue sharing funds (rejected, 102–302);
5. Housing and Community Development Amendments: Ritter amendment to transfer $200 million from the urban development grant program to the community development block grant program (rejected, 159–263);
6. Housing and Community Development Amendments: Neal amendment to make up to 20 percent of urban development action grant funds available to cities and urban counties that have at least one area of severe poverty (passed, 312–102);
7. Housing and Community Development Amendments: Hansen amendment to eliminate Davis-Bacon prevailing wage requirements for Indian housing and for housing rehabilitation projects carried out by neighborhood nonprofit organizations (rejected, 155–244);
8. Emergency Highway and Transportation Repair: Howard motion to

Table 7.5. Congressional Votes (Urban Issues), 1978

Variables	New York City Aid	EPA Appropriations	Chrysler Aid	Revenue Sharing	Community Development	Poverty Area Funds	Davis-Bacon Wage Requirements	Transit Repair	Education
Constant	-2.615	-5.227	9.567	-5.194	13.139	10.876	11.541	3.143	7.391
	(0.58)	(-0.86)	(2.16)[a]	(-0.93)	(2.07)[a]	(1.28)[a]	(2.41)[a]	(0.65)	(1.09)
Seniority	-0.006	-0.006	-0.265	0.022	-0.027	-0.035	-0.037	-0.146	-0.018
	(-0.29)	(-0.29)	(-1.51)[a]	(1.31)[a]	(-1.14)	(-1.72)[a]	(-1.88)[a]	(-0.84)	(-1.03)
Union members	-12.217	-5.726	-12.711	-19.328	-0.678	-21.628	-16.611	-21.397	11.814
	(-2.96)[a]	(-0.97)	(-3.58)[a]	(-5.15)[a]	(-0.13)	(-3.62)[a]	(-4.03)[a]	(-5.60)[a]	(3.26)[a]
Ford vote	0.061	0.057	0.015	0.039	0.089	0.040	0.022	-0.058	0.007
	(2.76)[a]	(2.75)[a]	(0.82)	(2.00)[a]	(2.40)[a]	(1.45)[a]	(0.98)	(2.85)[a]	(0.35)
ADA	-0.051	-0.049	-0.020	-0.013	-0.044	-0.029	-0.049	-0.016	-0.044
	(-4.10)[a]	(-2.89)[a]	(-1.86)[a]	(-1.22)	(-3.24)[a]	(-1.89)[a]	(-3.82)[a]	(-1.46)[a]	(-3.88)[a]
Electoral margin	0.030	0.056	-0.101	0.024	-0.175	-0.036	-0.109	-0.038	-0.099
	(0.76)	(1.05)	(-2.20)[a]	(0.64)	(-3.68)[a]	(-0.59)	(-2.58)[a]	(-0.91)	(-2.23)[a]
Labor contributions	0.037	0.045	-0.082	0.076	-0.192	-0.047	-0.099	-0.037	-0.091
	(1.28)[a]	(0.91)	(-1.23)	(2.65)[a]	(-5.39)[a]	(-1.05)	(-3.22)[a]	(-1.22)	(-3.05)[a]
Business contributions	0.018	0.096	-0.074	0.018	-0.162	0.021	-0.106	-0.048	-0.124
	(0.30)	(1.19)	(-1.23)	(0.32)	(-2.43)[a]	(0.22)	(-1.72)[a]	(-0.72)	(-1.97)[a]
Central city residents	-0.011	0.004	0.001	0.0016	-0.011	-0.012	0.012	0.001	0.028
	(-1.71)[a]	(0.57)	(0.26)	(0.52)	(-1.33)[a]	(-1.77)[a]	(1.81)[a]	(0.14)	(4.90)[a]
Dummy New York	-3.222	—	—	—	—	—	—	—	—
	(-2.94)[a]								
Cooperative contributions	-0.046	0.194	—	—	—	—	—	—	—
	(-0.35)	(0.56)							
Oil production	—	-0.056	-0.016	—	—	—	—	0.007	—
		(-2.64)[a]	(-0.91)					(0.37)	
Coal production	—	-0.013	—	—	—	—	—	—	—
		(-2.09)[a]							

	(1)	(2)	(3)	(4)	(5)	(6)	(7)	(8)	(9)
Medical contributions	—	-0.057 (-0.54)	—	—	—	—	—	—	—
% farmers	—	0.045 (0.48)	—	—	—	—	—	-0.723 (-2.16)[a]	—
% poverty	—	—	—	—	-0.003 (-0.06)	0.026 (0.58)	—	—	—
Dummy Michigan	—	—	-1.859 (-1.71)[a]	—	—	—	—	—	—
Defense spending	—	—	0.151 (0.35)	—	—	—	—	—	—
Federal spending	—	—	—	0.128 (0.39)	—	—	0.017 (1.09)	—	—
% black	—	—	—	-0.013 (-0.98)	0.027 (1.42)[a]	0.031 (2.09)[a]	—	—	—
Age	—	—	—	0.038 (0.82)	—	-0.126 (-1.88)[a]	—	—	0.012 (0.23)
Education	—	—	—	—	-0.266 (-0.09)	—	—	—	0.088 (0.48)
HUD spending	—	—	—	—	10.053 (0.72)	—	—	—	—
HEW spending	—	—	—	—	—	2.484 (1.16)	—	—	0.466 (0.28)
Consumers	—	—	—	—	—	—	0.034 (0.94)	-0.008 (-0.21)	-0.011 (-0.31)
R^2	.38	.33	.20	.10	.51	.40	.39	.19	.25
Correct forecast	.81	.77	.74	.76	.87	.86	.83	.75	.74

Note: t-values in parentheses.
[a] Significant at the 0.10 level.

Table 7.6. Determinants of Contributions (Urban Issues), 1978

Contributions	Constant	Party 1 = Dem. 0 = Rep.	Loser's Total Contributions	Dummy Primary	Seniority	Vote Index	R²
Business contributions	12.946 (10.56)ᵃ	-3.476 (-2.37)ᵃ	0.040 (4.25)ᵃ	4.740 (3.89)ᵃ	0.035 (0.49)	8.429 (5.94)ᵃ	0.28
Individual contributions	22.158 (5.98)ᵃ	12.322 (2.76)ᵃ	0.210 (7.43)ᵃ	12.133 (3.27)ᵃ	-0.618 (-2.88)ᵃ	17.612 (4.03)ᵃ	0.27
Labor contributions	3.758 (2.70)ᵃ	4.76 (2.85)ᵃ	0.101 (9.52)ᵃ	-2.564 (-1.84)ᵃ	-0.105 (-1.31)ᵃ	-13.721 (-8.39)ᵃ	0.42
Party contributions	14.463 (20.86)ᵃ	-12.565 (-20.72)ᵃ	0.058 (10.40)ᵃ	3.143 (4.27)ᵃ	-0.183 (-4.31)ᵃ		0.60
Medical contributions	14.574 (11.595)ᵃ	-0.096 (-0.06)	0.028 (2.97)ᵃ	3.444 (2.75)ᵃ	-0.024 (-0.33)	10.911 (7.40)ᵃ	0.26
Cooperative contributions	0.0756 (2.64)ᵃ	1.810 (5.29)ᵃ	-0.001 (-0.63)	-0.138 (-0.48)	-0.037 (-2.25)ᵃ	1.37 (4.09)ᵃ	0.07

Note: t-values in parentheses.
ᵃSignificant at the 0.10 level.

Table 7.7. Determinants of Electoral
Margin (Urban Issues), 1978

Variables	Margin
Constant term	75.543
	(30.54)[a]
Incumbent	-2.190
	(-0.85)
Loser's total contributions	-0.114
	(-9.26)[a]
Winner's total contributions	-0.035
	(-2.91)[a]
Seniority	-0.079
	(-0.97)
DOD (VI)	-9.124
	(-1.08)
Coal production (VI)	0.014
	(0.31)
Oil production (VI)	0.114
	(0.61)
Age (VI)	0.262
	(0.58)
Ford vote (VI)	0.533
	(3.77)[a]
% black (VI)	0.151
	(1.58)[a]
Consumers (VI)	-1.023
	(-1.85)[a]
% union members (VI)	-30.72
	(-0.60)
Education	3.88
	(1.93)[a]
HEW spending (VI)	-20.12
	(-0.92)
Federal spending (VI)	6.715
	(0.93)
% farmers (VI)	-0.124
	(-0.30)
Central city residents (VI)	-0.036
	(-0.84)
Poverty (VI)	0.200
	(-0.45)
HUD spending (VI)	-2.814
	(-0.02)
R^2	0.41

Note: t-values in parentheses.
[a]t-values significant at the 0.10 level.

    authorize $250 million to reimburse the states 100 percent for the cost of repairing weather-related damage to transportation systems (passed, 274–137);

9.   Education Department: adoption of the conference committee report to create the Department of Education (passed, 215–201).

    The results for the simultaneous estimation process are reported in tables 7.5, 7.6, and 7.7. Comparing these tables with tables 7.2, 7.3, and 7.4, we see that the results are very similar. The major differences are that some of the interest groups seem to have more impact on voting on urban bills than on general bills. Union contributions remain more often significant than business contributions, and, in general, the pattern of results does not change. The determinants of electoral margin and of contributions is almost identical between the two sets of votes. We have defined the votes so that the Ford vote in a district receives a *positive* sign; as in the first set of votes (see table 7.2), we observe unions almost invariably opposed to Ford in the voting. The consistency between tables 7.2, 7.3, and 7.4 and tables 7.5, 7.6, and 7.7 indicates that the particular set of bills chosen to estimate the general equilibrium system is probably not significant; we would expect to get about the same results for any reasonably broad set of bills. (It is impossible to estimate more than eight or nine bills at a time because of econometric limitations; thus the consistency we have found is encouraging because it shows that our results are rather robust and that a small number of bills is sufficient for detection of patterns in legislation).

    In this chapter we have tested the theoretical model relating voting by representatives, voting for representatives by constituents, and contributions to representatives by donors. We have hypothesized voting by representatives to be a function of constituent characteristics and campaign contributions; voting by constituents for representatives, a function of the representative's stand on bills affecting constituents, of seniority of the representative, and of money spent in the election campaign; contributions by donors, a function of a representative's seniority and voting behavior. We have empirically tested this model using a simultaneous equations logit model. In general, the results support the specification.

    Our main purpose in undertaking this research was not to understand the electoral process, an area of inquiry where political scientists presumably have a comparative advantage. Rather, we were attempting to find out which interest groups have favored which laws because economists must understand the nature of the forces that lead to passage of laws with substantial economic implications. Our primary concern has been to determine the impetus for laws that serve to increase government regulation of the economy. Our results have indicated that (1) much of the force behind regulatory laws may come from ideology, and (2) unions seem to be active in the political sector of the economy and seem to favor increased regulation and intervention; business seems to oppose such governmental actions. By estimating the system for two sets of laws, we have been able to determine that our results seem quite robust.[5]

NOTES

1. Sources: Data on income, central city residents, percentage of blacks, education, age, percentage of farmers, government spending, seniority, party, and electoral margin are from the *Almanac of American Politics* (1978). Data on union membership are from the U.S. Department of Labor (1975); on oil production, from the American Petroleum Institute (1975); on coal production, from the U.S. Bureau of Mines (1975). Data on roll call voting are from the *Congressional Quarterly*, various issues. Data on contributions are from the Federal Election Commission (1979).

2. All votes were transformed so that a vote for relatively more government was a "yes" vote, and a vote for relatively less government was a "no" vote. Thus, the effect of voting for Ford in the Ford-Carter election was always negative.

3. The R^2's in table 7.2 are a measure of the empirical information provided by the model and are computed as $\frac{1}{M} \sum_i \sum_j \delta_{ij} \log \frac{\hat{P}_{ij}}{P(y_j)}$, where $\hat{P}_{ij}$ is the predicted probability from the model and $P(y_j)$ is a selected prior distribution. Here the priors are total uncertainty (i.e., equally likely alternatives) and the market-share hypothesis. The value may be interpreted as the percent of uncertainty explained by the model (see Hauser 1977).

4. The predicted values were transformed by 2 times the predicted value minus 1. This resulted in a continuous distribution from $+1$ to -1.

5. We have also performed the same estimation, with Ford voting but without the ADA rating, for both the general set of votes and for the urban votes. The results are similar but not quite as good. However, in these estimations we find that Ford is always significant. Otherwise, the pattern of the results does not change radically.

III CONTRIBUTIONS

8 A COMPARISON OF THE 1972 AND 1978 ELECTIONS: *Role of the PACs*

Chapter 7 dealt with an analysis of the 1978 congressional election. In that election political action committees (PACs) were more active than in any previous election (though not as active as they were in 1980). In this chapter we examine the role of these committees in influencing legislation by comparing the results of the estimation for 1978 with results of a similar (though less complete) examination of the 1972 congressional election. By focusing on the differing roles of political contributions in these two elections, we can determine the extent to which legislative changes in campaign financing laws had an impact. Before presenting the comparison, however, we should first consider the legislation that affected the role of political action committees.

THE FEDERAL ELECTION CAMPAIGN ACT

Current regulations of spending on political campaigns are the result of the 1971 Federal Election Campaign Act (FECA), 1974 and 1975 amendments to the act, major Supreme Court decisions (*Pipefitters Local 562* v. *United States* and *Buckley* v. *Valeo*), and the rulings of the Federal Election Commission in the SUN-PAC case. The following discussion of the FECA and of the other amendments and decisions is based on Epstein (1979).

Perhaps the most interesting feature of the electoral reform begun with the 1971 FECA is that the result is apparently almost exactly opposite from what the supporters of electoral reform desired. The law was backed primarily by unions and by Democrats who wanted to secure unions' ability to contribute to political campaigns; the resulting legislation, however, has enabled businesses to contribute more heavily than before to political activities. The proponents of the law were not alone in their surprise at the outcome; academic commentators also believed that the law would primarily help labor unions and their allies. Posner (1977), for example, argued that the act would serve to benefit interest groups that contributed in kind rather than in money. Abrams and Settle (1978) argued that the law would serve to benefit Democrats (the party in power when the law was passed) at the expense of Republicans. Epstein concludes that the supporters of the law were erroneous in their forecasts and may have been net losers from the law's passage.

The history of the FECA and its relation to political action committees may be summarized as follows: In 1971 Congress was debating a law regulating campaign spending. At the same time the *Pipefitters Local 562* case was before the Supreme Court. Had the United States won this case, the ability of unions to continue to contribute to election campaigns would have been seriously weakened. As insurance against such a verdict, the AFL-CIO requested Representative Hansen to introduce a bill that allowed unions to form PACs. The bill also allowed businesses to form PACs, but the bill's supporters felt that businesses would not take advantage of this right. However, after passage of the bill, about eighty business PACs were established and became involved in the 1972 election.

In 1974 the FECA was amended in an attempt to limit the influence of campaign contributions on public policy. One important modification was the establishment of the Federal Election Commission (FEC) to administer the law; another was explicit permission for government contractors to contribute to campaigns. This amendment was passed, again at the behest of unions, which wanted to guarantee their right to continue to contribute to campaigns. And once again the impact of the amendment was probably exactly counter to what supporters intended, especially after the FEC advisory opinion in the 1975 SUN-PAC case: The FEC ruled that Sun Oil could use corporate funds to set up a PAC, could solicit contributions from both stockholders and employees, and could establish multiple PACs with separate limits.

The 1976 Supreme Court decision in *Buckley* v. *Valeo*, based largely on First Amendment grounds of free speech, further expanded the rights of corporations to solicit contributions. The decision also removed spending limits, provided that overspending by a PAC was independent of the campaign of the benefited candidate. The 1976 amendments to the FECA somewhat limited the ability of businesses to use PACs, but the net result of the legislation clearly increased the power of corporations and businesses to contribute to political campaigns. The fact that the supporters of campaign spending reform intended the opposite result may say something about the predictability of the political process; the fact that academic commentators were also misled may say something about the ability of economists and other academics to predict political outcomes.

THE 1972 ELECTION

In chapter 7 we examined the 1978 election, the first congressional election to occur after full legislative enactment of campaign finance reform. In this chapter we examine the 1972 congressional election. PACs had some slight influence in 1972, but not nearly so much influence as they seem to have had in later elections. Thus, by comparing the results in 1972 and 1978, we can perhaps discover something about the impact of laws dealing with campaign financing reform. We proceed here exactly as we did in chapter 7: We specify and test the general equilibrium model of congressional voting in order to determine the impact of various factors on congressional voting. However, the data used here are not the same as the data used earlier; in particular, we do not have data on contributions received by the loser in the election, so we have a potential specification problem. Also, the 1972 data (gathered by Common Cause) are less complete than the data for 1978 (gathered by the FEC); in particular, 1972 business contributions do not include contributions from individuals associated with business, and 1972 union contributions do not include contributions in kind from unions. Nonetheless, the comparison may tell us something of interest.

First is the simple issue of magnitude. We saw in table 7.1 that business contributed $5.3 million and unions contributed $4.7 million in 1978. In 1972 the order of these magnitudes was reversed: Unions contributed $3.6 million, and business, $1.7 million. (As indicated, both of these figures are incomplete.)

To determine the effect of these contributions, we have again estimated a general equilibrium model. The estimation procedures are essentially the same as those used in chapter 7. We have chosen a sample of seven bills for 1973–74, the years in which the representatives elected in 1972 were in office. The bills are as follows:

Table 8.1. Determinants of Congressional Voting, 1972

Variables	Minimum Wage	Toxic Substances	Federal Salaries	Emergency Petroleum Allocation	Wage-Price Controls	OSHA	Consumer Protection Agency
Constant term	14.091 (2.53)a	-8.025 (1.51)a	-9.976 (-3.03)a	-2.545 (-0.80)	-19.706 (-3.10)a	-11.097 (-2.97)a	-7.199 (-2.14)a
Seniority	-0.0128 (-0.43)	-0.0613 (-2.40)a	0.0102 (0.43)	-0.035 (-1.50)a	-0.0875 (-3.15)a	-0.0165 (-0.62)	-0.0199 (-0.78)
Nixon vote	-0.1012 (4.53)a	0.1039 (6.10)a	-0.0568 (-3.89)a	0.0944 (4.93)a	-0.0583 (-3.82)a	0.1903 (7.63)a	0.1231 (5.70)a
% union members	0.0465 (2.04)a	0.0359 (1.96)a	0.0667 (3.51)a	—	-0.0037 (-0.18)	-0.0706 (-2.99)a	-0.0290 (-1.36)a
% black	-0.0245 (-1.34)a	—	0.0080 (0.53)	—	-0.0586 (-4.09)a	—	-0.0057 (-0.32)
Consumers	-0.1872 (-1.97)a	-0.1437 (-1.76)a	—	-0.1100 (-1.51)a	—	0.1503 (1.32)a	-0.1380 (-1.69)a
% auto employment	-0.0023 (-3.59)a	—	—	0.00095 (1.90)a	—	0.0017 (2.45)a	0.00013 (0.21)
HEW spending	0.0062 (2.89)a	—	—	—	—	—	—
Education	-0.6259 (-2.55)a	0.3444 (1.60)a	—	—	0.3440 (1.59)a	—	—
% farmers	—	0.2760 (2.82)a	—	—	—	-0.0898 (-0.73)	—

Age	—	−0.1597 (−3.53)[a]	—	—	0.0484 (0.92)	—	—
Federal spending	—	—	0.0013 (3.88)[a]	—	—	—	—
% airline employees	—	—	−0.0026 (−2.26)[a]	0.00094 (0.70)	—	—	—
Oil production	—	—	—	0.0015 (5.33)[a]	—	—	—
Coal production	—	—	—	−0.0003 (−0.52)	—	—	—
Central city residents	—	—	—	−0.0012 (−0.19)	—	—	—
Business contributions	−0.0001 (−0.44)	0.0034 (1.76)[a]	0.00042 (2.30)[a]	−0.00018 (−0.81)	0.00019 (1.06)	−0.00019 (−0.83)	0.00044 (2.33)[a]
Union contributions	0.00045 (6.84)[a]	−0.00007 (−0.86)	0.00027 (5.64)[a]	−0.00019 (−3.39)[a]	0.00051 (9.30)[a]	−0.00049 (−4.84)[a]	−0.00033 (−5.83)[a]
Agricultural contributions	−0.00083 (−3.68)[a]	−0.00091 (−1.80)[a]	−0.00041 (−2.35)[a]	−0.0398 (−1.07)	−0.00077 (−3.93)[a]	0.00082 (1.24)	0.00024 (1.15)
Electoral margin	−0.0119 (−0.03)	0.0560 (1.58)[a]	0.1262 (3.21)[a]	0.000025 (0.14)	0.2354 (5.02)[a]	0.0139 (0.36)	0.0093 (0.25)
Correct forecast	0.82	0.76	0.80	0.77	0.85	0.86	0.83
R^2	0.48	0.33	0.33	0.37	0.48	0.52	0.46

[a] t-values significant at the 0.05 level for two-tailed tests.

1. Minimum Wage: final passage of the bill to increase the minimum wage and extend coverage (passed, 287–130, in 1973);
2. Toxic Substances: amendment to require the administrator of the Environmental Protection Agency to hold hearings and allow cross-examination of witnesses; this bill would have weakened the power of the EPA to regulate toxic substances (rejected, 159–236, in 1973);
3. Federal Salaries: bill to increase federal salaries (including those of Congress, the cabinet, and the judiciary) and provide for review of such salaries every two years rather than every four years (rejected, 156–237, in 1973);
4. Emergency Petroleum Allocation: bill to provide that allocation of crude oil would occur at the pipeline but not at the production stage; it would have weakened federal controls over oil (rejected, 136–245, in 1973);
5. Wage-Price Controls Extension: bill to strengthen the president's power to control wages and prices (rejected, 151–253, in 1973);
6. OSHA Appropriations: bill to reduce appropriations for the Occupational Safety and Health Administration (rejected, 179–217, in 1974);
7. Consumer Protection Agency: bill to limit the CPA's right of judicial review; it would have weakened the agency (rejected, 149–251, in 1974).

As in chapter 7, econometric techniques were greatly simplified by having the same number of votes on each bill; thus, we assigned votes to each non-voting representative on the basis of the votes of the majority of other representatives from the same state. Where a tie made such assignment impossible, a random process was used.

The results of the estimation procedure are reported in tables 8.1, 8.2, and 8.3. The nature of the results should by now be familiar. The ideological variable, voting in the Nixon-McGovern election in the congressional district, is always significant. Union membership is often significant; other constituent characteristics are sometimes significant. Business contributions are significant in three of seven votes, and union contributions are significant in six of seven. Agricultural contributions are significant four times. Union contributions are always associated with voting for relatively more government (i.e., union contributions always have a sign opposite to the Nixon vote when significant), and business contributions have no clear pattern. Surprisingly, the role of business contributions in influencing congressional voting appears unchanged from 1972 to 1978; in neither year were business contributions very important. Union contributions, however, were

Table 8.2.   Determinants of Contributions, 1972

	Constant	Party	Seniority	Vote Index	R^2	d.f.
Business	2926.45	−1693.82	18.466	14.480	0.11	431
contributions	(14.13)[a]	(−6.91)[a]	(1.31)	(0.06)		
Agricultural	771.29	585.06	−29.77	707.25	0.06	431
contributions	(5.18)[a]	(3.32)[a]	(−2.94)[a]	(4.01)[a]		
Union	1560.04	6078.28	−129.91	−2284.23	0.33	431
contributions	(3.63)[a]	(11.96)[a]	(−4.46)[a]	(−4.49)[a]		

[a]t-values significant at the 0.05 level for a two-tailed test.

significant in both years. Thus, the results indicate that as of 1978, business PACs had no major influence on voting by representatives.

In table 8.2 we observe an important difference from the 1978 results. In 1972 no relationship existed between the vote index (the measure of liberalism or conservatism of the representative) and the amount of contributions received from business. In 1978, for both specifications, we do find such an influence. In 1972 business gave to candidates independently of their ideological orientation; in 1978 business gave primarily to conservative candidates. (The data and variables for 1972 are less complete than those for 1978; however, we do observe that in 1972 agricultural contributors gave to conservative candidates and unions gave to liberal candidates. Thus, the insignificance of ideological interests in influencing business contributions is probably not due to data problems.) An interest group might give to a candidate for two reasons. First, the aim of the group might be to change the way in which the candidate will vote if elected. Second, the group might try to elect candidates who would be expected to vote as the group desired. The simultaneous procedure that we use here can separate these two elements. We see that in 1978 business gave to candidates who would be expected to vote as business would like; however, business contributions did not influence the voting of these candidates. In 1972 business contributions were not even related to the voting pattern of the candidate. Thus, the effect of the law was to channel business contributions toward candidates who were favorable to business interests. In contrast, unions were giving to liberal (i.e., progovernment) candidates as early as 1972 and were able to influence the way in which recipient candidates voted. What we may be observing is a learning process on the part of business contributors; that is, unions have had more experience in contributing to campaigns than business has had and thus may be more successful. If this theory is correct, we can expect business

Table 8.3. Determinants of Constituent Voting, 1972

Variables	Margin
Constant term	59.948
	(34.73)[a]
Contributions	−0.000179
	(−0.66)
Seniority	0.547
	(7.26)[a]
V. Nixon vote	0.612
	(5.26)[a]
V. % blacks	−0.0485
	(−2.56)[a]
V. Consumers	−0.0307
	(−0.04)
V. Union members	0.0995
	(0.36)
V. Education	−1.628
	(−1.12)
V. HEW spending	0.021
	(0.82)
V. Auto employment	0.772
	(0.10)
V. Federal spending	0.0057
	(2.88)[a]
V. Farmers	−0.0784
	(−0.19)
V. Oil production	−0.00053
	(−0.31)
V. Central city residents	−0.0211
	(−0.42)
V. Age	−0.0612
	(−0.12)
V. Coal production	0.00003
	(0.51)
V. Airline employment	−10.604
	(−0.08)
R^2	0.22
d.f.	418

[a]t-values significant at the 0.05 level.

to be more successful in the future at influencing the voting behavior of re-cipients of their contributions.

Table 8.3 indicates that contributions were insignificant in explaining voting by constituents. However, this table is incomplete because we have no data on loser contributions (a variable that is always significant in explaining constituent voting); thus, we should view the results with some caution.

In sum, important changes took place in campaign finance law between 1972 and 1978. By examining in detail the influence of contributions on the elections of these two years, we are able to determine some of the impact of campaign finance laws, which seem in general to have increased the ability of businesses and corporations to contribute to electoral campaigns. We find that in 1972 no relationship was apparent between the ideological voting of a representative and the amount of contributions he or she received from business; nor did any relationship exist between voting and contributions received. That is, in 1972 business gave almost at random to representatives, and business contributions had no impact. In 1978 business gave to conser-vative representatives, but business contributions still had no influence on the voting of these recipients. In contrast, in both years unions gave to liberal representatives, and the recipients of union contributions became signifi-cantly more liberal as a result of receiving these contributions. The evidence indicates that changes in the law have benefited business relatively more than unions; thus, in supporting the 1972 FECA and its amendments in 1974 and 1976, unions were actually going against their own self-interest in the long run. Moreover, because the financing changes have changed the composi-tion of Congress, we probably will not see a return to the earlier campaign finance regulations.

9 SOME ADDITIONAL EFFECTS OF CONTRIBUTIONS

In this chapter we examine some additional implications of the importance of contributions to political campaigns. In chapters 7 and 8 we showed that contributions could affect the way in which representatives vote. That is, contributions could be used not only to elect representatives who would vote as the contributor desired, but also to influence the way in which elected representatives would choose to vote. In this chapter we examine two issues related to the impact of contributions on voting changes. First, to determine the actual effect of certain selected types of contributions, we ask what the Congress would have been like if these contributions had not been made. Second, we ask how much it would have cost various contributors to shift congressional voting in desired directions. That is, we ask: "What is the 'price' of Congress?"

In this examination we use the voting results for 1978, the year used in chapter 7. We also use the results in chapter 7 of the first set of estimations, in which we were concerned with a general set of issues. In this chapter we use as our variable the vote index (VI) rather than voting on individual bills. That is, we define an index of liberal-conservative voting by Congress on the eight bills examined in table 7.2. The index is defined to take a value of 1 for complete liberalism and 0 for complete conservatism. That is, a representative who always voted for increased government intervention (i.e., who always voted as did Carter voters) would have an index value of 1, and a representative who always voted for decreased intervention would have a score of 0. We have essentially duplicated the sort of index constructed by the ADA and other such groups, but we have used the eight votes previously examined in chapter 7 rather than the votes used by these groups. However, as shown in chapter 6, high correlations exist between any of these indices, so our results should not depend on the set of votes that we have selected.

We then proceed to estimate a simultaneous system like the one estimated in chapter 7; however, instead of having one equation for each of eight votes, we now have one equation for the liberalism index. This equation is reported in table 9.1. The results of this estimation are consistent with the results reported in chapter 7 for voting on each bill. The significant variables are central city residents, Ford voting, union contributions, and medical contributions, with the expected sign on each. Each coefficient represents the amount of change in liberalism for each unit change in the variable. For example, the coefficient associated with union contributions, 0.0149, indicates that for each union contribution of $1,000, the average liberalism score increases by 0.0149. The results indicate that union contributions increase liberalism and medical contributions increase conservatism; contributions from business have no impact, a result consistent with the results found in chapter 7.

We may also compare the actual voting record of Congress with the predicted voting record without the two types of contributions that were significant in explaining voting. Thus, the actual average score of Congress is 0.467; without union contributions the score we predict is 0.294, a significantly more conservative score. Without medical contributions we predict a score of 0.801, a significantly more liberal rating. This is one way of indicating the influence of campaign contributions on the policies adopted by Congress.

Another way of indicating the same result is shown in table 9.2. Here we provide estimates of the cost to union and medical contributors of moving Congress to various desired levels of liberalism or conservatism. Thus, for example, if unions wanted a liberalism score of 0.75 (instead of the actual score of 0.467), they would have had to contribute an average of $28,890 per representative, for a total contribution of $12,567,327. Medical contributors would have had to donate in the same way to achieve various conservatism scores. The projected required contributions are from a structural equation similar to the voting equations used in chapter 7. The dependent variable is an index structured from the votes used in the 1978 results. The independent variables are the same as those used in the separate voting equations. The

Table 9.1. Determinants of the Vote Index, 1978

Variables	Vote Index
Constant term	1.296
	(1.47)
Seniority	0.00254
	(0.89)
Central city residents	0.00173
	(2.82)[a]
Education	−0.0329
	(−0.78)
Defense spending	−0.00737
	(−0.19)
HEW spending	0.1866
	(1.00)
% farmers	−0.00169
	(−0.09)
% black	−0.0023
	(−1.45)[a]
Ford vote	−0.0064
	(−2.28)[a]
Oil production	−0.0023
	(−0.75)
Coal production	−0.000789
	(0.99)
Business contributions	0.0033
	(0.35)
Union contributions	0.0149
	(2.72)[a]
Cooperative contributions	0.0172
	(0.22)
Medical contributions	−0.0248
	(−1.95)[a]
Electoral margin	−0.0016
	(−0.28)
% union members	0.1803
	(0.26)
R^2	0.68

Note: 1.00 = Liberal.
[a]Significant at the 0.10 level.

Table 9.2. Union and Medical Contributions Required to Move Congress
to Various Levels of Liberalism and Conservatism

	Desired Level, Union Contributors			Desired Level, Medical Contributors		
	1.00	*0.75*	*0.50*	*0.00*	*0.25*	*0.50*
Total contribution	$44,602	$28,890	$14,099	$34,794	$23,928	$13,159
	$19,402,209	$12,567,327	$6,133,339	$15,135,396	$10,408,779	$5,724,264

Note: 1.00 = Liberal.

predicted values in the estimation reflect the movement from one equilibrium to another with a change in contributions. The contributions are not forecast (predict values), but are instead the amount required to move from one equilibrium to another.

Notice that we predict that moving the Congress to a level of 0.5 liberalism would require union contributions of $6,133,339 and medical contributions of $5,724,264. The actual level of liberalism in Congress was 0.467, slightly below 0.5. Actual union contributions (see table 7.1) were $4,760,007, and actual medical contributions were $6,296,080, values close to the values predicted to be required to achieve a level of 0.5. Thus, the model seems to fit the actual data rather well.

We have provided an estimate of the cost of moving the entire Congress from one level of liberalism or conservatism to another level. It would also be possible to provide similar estimates for each representative; that is, we could estimate the cost of moving each representative to a more or less liberal position. We could also provide similar estimates for particular issues — for example, we could provide the cost of making Congress more or less favorable to issues affecting any given industry. In addition, we could generate breakdowns by individual and issue and could generate the cost of making a certain representative more favorable to a certain industry group. Thus, the types of estimation procedures we have used could be used to provide the "price" of Congress or of a representative.

One caveat should be noted in connection with the results presented here: We have dealt solely with the cost of changing the position of elected representatives. However, an interest group might also choose to use its contributions to elect representatives who are favorable to its position. For reasons discussed in chapter 7, the estimation procedures and data available to us are unable to determine the effects of this type of spending.

10 CONCLUSIONS AND IMPLICATIONS

CONCLUSIONS

We began with the question of the determinants of recent regulatory legislation, much of which does not seem explicable in terms of the now standard economic theory of regulation (i.e., regulation is bought and sold, with special-interest groups as the buyers and legislatures as the sellers). In many cases the new regulation makes it difficult or impossible to identify a beneficiary; beneficiaries that can be identified do not seem to fit the normally understood definition of special-interest groups. Moreover, the amount of new regulatory legislation argues against its being the result of simple, random errors. Thus, explaining this legislation is a challenge to economists.

One conclusion of our work — perhaps the strongest conclusion — is that ideology appears to be the explanation for much of the new legislation. We have measured ideology in several ways — by membership in public interest lobbies, by ADA ratings earned by representatives, and by voting in congressional districts in recent presidential elections. In all cases the ideological variable is by far the strongest and most significant variable in explaining congressional voting, even after numerous attempts to adjust

121

statistically for economic interests of constituents and campaign contributors. Our results may possibly be wrong — no one can prove a scientific result — but the weight of evidence we have summarized is such that the burden of proof has shifted. Those who claim that economic factors are the basis of all legislation should be required to document their claim. It is no longer sufficient merely to argue that the lack of an economic explanation for some law is the result of the failure of the analyst to identify the relevant interest groups; the one who claims that an economic explanation exists must be challenged to discover the interest group that benefits.

In the process of testing the hypothesis that ideology is an explanation for congressional voting, we developed and tested a very general model of the legislative process. It seems useful to gather in one place all the implications that we have generated about interest groups of various sorts.

First, unions seem to be the most efficient actors in the political process. The number of union members in the district is generally associated with voting by the representative in the predicted direction. Union contributions also seem generally significant in explaining congressional voting. Moreover, unions invariably take stands in favor of more government intervention of all sorts. In some cases we can explain union desire for such intervention in terms of the interests of union members — for example, unions support minimum wages that increase relative demand for their highly paid, highly skilled members. In other cases, however (e.g., imposition of wage-price controls), it is difficult to explain union interest in greater regulation, even though such an interest is clearly demonstrated by the data. Moreover, unions use their campaign funds both to elect relatively liberal representatives and to change the voting pattern of elected representatives in a more liberal direction. That is, if we ask whether unions give to liberal representatives or whether the receipt of union contributions makes representatives more liberal, we find that both occur.

Second, businesses as political contributors seem less skilled than unions. In 1972 business seemed to contribute randomly to political campaigns; in 1978, even after their political action committees had grown substantially and had channeled contributions to conservative representatives, businesses were unable to influence many votes of the recipients of campaign funds. Business may still be learning to maximize the impact of their campaign contributions, but our evidence indicates that, at least as of 1978, business was not as skilled at using campaign contributions as were unions.

Another result of our research is that, except for union members, not many constituent interest groups seem to have much influence on the legislative process. Central city residents are more often significant than most other groups and, when significant, urban residents tend to be liberal.

Blacks are not often significant; when significant, they are likely to be conservative. Educated people seem split between liberalism and conservatism. Consumer interests, as represented by membership in Consumers' Union, seem generally liberal except on issues that serve directly to raise consumer prices. Perhaps most surprisingly, government spending in a congressional district does not generally seem significant, whether we aggregate government spending into total spending or disaggregate it into defense spending, HEW spending, and other spending. In general, even in bills of direct interest to government employees, the spending variables are not significant. Moreover, the lack of significance of constituent variables is probably not due to data or econometric problems because one aspect of constituent characteristics, the liberalism or conservatism of voters (measured by the vote in presidential elections), is highly significant in explaining voting by members of Congress. Economic interests of constituents are less significant than one would have expected.

Finally, we have developed information on the impact of campaign contributions on roll call voting, and we find that it is possible to use such contributions to change votes. Not only can contributions help elect representatives who favor the position of the donors, but contributions can also help change the positions of elected representatives. As we have seen, unions seemed (as of 1978) better than business at manipulating voting through contributions, but in principle both groups should be able to accomplish this goal.

IMPLICATIONS FOR FUTURE RESEARCH

This research could be extended in various ways. In terms of the variables, the major weakness is that we do not have an independent measure of relative strength of candidates before campaigning begins. In our estimation of the equations for electoral margin, we find that spending by both the winner and the loser is associated with a smaller margin for the winner because winners must spend more if they face strong challengers but are unable fully to counter the advantage of strong challengers. Jacobson (1980) tried to measure the strength of the challenger by including a variable that measured whether or not the challenger had ever held electoral office, but this measure of strength was not sufficient. Ideally, we would probably want results of political polls at the beginning of the campaign for each congressional district. Absent this variable, some other measure of relative strength would be necessary to specify correctly the equation relating campaign contributions to voting by constituents for representatives.

Other extensions of our analysis are possible. For example, we have examined only the House of Representatives; similar analyses could be performed for the Senate. It would also be possible to examine other areas of voting, such as foreign policy–related issues. Perhaps more importantly, the results could be extended in time. For example, popular press reports have indicated that contributions from various types of PACs were more important in the 1980 election than in past elections; thus, the type of analysis used here should be able to determine the degree of influence such contributions have had on the voting patterns of the 1980 Congress. Moreover, by comparing results from 1972 to 1980, we should be able to develop new evidence or predict new trends.

It is also possible to make a prediction based on these results. The 1980 election of Ronald Reagan seems to indicate that voters have become more conservative. Our evidence indicates that greater voter conservatism should lead to congressional voting for significantly less government intervention. Other theories of politics hold that the election of one candidate rather than another should have no impact on the power of special interests; therefore, the election of 1980 should have little impact on government intervention. Thus, an independent evaluation of our research may be made by studying the direction in which the 1980 Congress moves.

The results of our research also have implications for economics as a discipline. Stigler's (1980) theory — that laws are passed solely as a result of self-interest — leaves virtually no scope for economists to influence policy. He maintains that policies are passed as result of the ability of groups with sufficient political power to obtain legislation that benefits them; the arguments of economists and other social scientists about the merits of legislation therefore carry no weight. Our results indicate substantially more scope for social scientists to influence legislation because ideology, which we find influential in the passage of legislation, is the product of social scientists. Thus, the results that indicate that noneconomic factors are important in influencing public policy serve somewhat to weaken the ability of economists to use strictly economic models to explain public policy. The same results, however, indicate that economists have substantial power to influence actual policy decisions.

APPENDIX:
Analysis of Econometric Models with Qualitative Dependent Variables

Economists have traditionally dealt with models designed to explain the variation in a dependent variable that could be assumed continuous and normally distributed. Economics, however, as a theory of choice, can be applied not only to questions about how much to produce or consume, but also to the question of *whether* to produce or consume a certain item. More generally, individual economic units often must choose between a finite set of alternatives. Economists are interested in determining what factors were considered by the decision-making unit and in quantifying the individual effects of those factors. Some examples of situations where choices arise are the following: (1) A household must decide whether to buy or rent a suitable dwelling; (2) a senator or representative must decide whether to vote yes or no on a particular piece of legislation; (3) a consumer must choose to visit one of several shopping areas and decide upon a mode of transportation; (4) members of a household must decide whether to take part-time or full-time employment or whether to seek a second job; (5) a person must decide whether or not to attend college. While the list could go on, the basic similarity of these situations is clear: In each case the decisionmaker must choose an action from a finite set of discrete alternatives (often two — for example, a yes-no decision). In this appendix we consider the difficulties associated with using traditional statistical techniques when dependent variables are qualitative. We present special models that are useful when dependent variables are qualitative, as well as a discussion of some computational methods that are employed with them.

A FRAMEWORK FOR STUDYING MODELS WITH BINARY DEPENDENT VARIABLES

When considering models in which the dependent variable can take only two values (e.g., $y_i = 1$ if an event E occurs, but $y_i = 0$ if the event does not occur), we must couch our discussion in terms of the probability of the event E occurring. Economic theory suggests a set of variables or factors that will be considered when a choice is to be made. However, we know that different individuals faced with identical circumstances and choices will often choose differently, based on their own preference structure. Moreover, a single individual will often make different choices in apparently identical situations. We can explain this phenomenon either by calling the choices intrinsic random human behavior or by concluding that the situations were not, in fact, identical and that changes in other unconsidered or omitted factors caused the variations in choice. Consequently, as in other statistical models, the outcome of a choice experiment is random, and thus y_i is random. In regression situations we assume that the expected value of the dependent variable is a function of a set of explanatory variables. The same will be true here, as we assume that the Bernoulli random variable y_i has expectation $E(y_i) = P_i$, where P_i is the probability that the event occurs. As economists, we are interested in factors that affect P_i. Thus, we assume P_i is a function of a set of explanatory variables, and from knowledge of the values of those variables and observations on the values taken by y_i, we estimate the parameters of the assumed functional relationship.

Each of the models we describe differs in its assumption about the relation between P_i and the explanatory variables. As a first step, we might assume that P_i is a linear function of a set of explanatory variables. That is, let $Ey_i = P_i = x_i'\beta$, where x_i' is a $1 \times K$ vector of observations on a set of explanatory variables and $\beta = (\beta_1, \ldots, \beta_K)'$ is the associated parameter vector. If then, as usual, we add a disturbance to account for the difference between the value of the observed random variable y_i and its mean $Ey_i = P_i$, we have

$$y_i = P_i + e_i = x_i'\beta + e_i \qquad i = 1, \ldots, T, \tag{A.1}$$

where T is the number of times the choice experiment is repeated. Since the dependent variable y_i can take only two values, the same is true of the error term e_i. The error term e_i takes the values

y_i	e_i	$Pr(e_i)$
1	$1 - x_i'\beta$	$(x_i'\beta)$
0	$-x_i'\beta$	$(1 - x_i'\beta),$

$$(A.2)$$

$1 - x_i'\beta$ and $-x_i'\beta$ when y_i takes the values 1 and 0, respectively. Furthermore, if we are to maintain the assumption that $E(e_i) = 0$ so that $E(y_i) = x_i'\beta$, then the values of e_i must have probabilities as shown in model A.2 since

$$E(e_i) = \sum_{i=1}^{2} e_i Pr(e_i)$$

$$= (1 - x_i'\beta)(x_i'\beta) + (-x_i'\beta)(1 - x_i'\beta) = 0.$$

The expectation $E(y_i) = P_i = x_i'\beta$ is now interpreted as the conditional probability, given x_i, that the event E occurs. From this point of view, and that in model A.2, the model A.1 is awkward since $x_i'\beta$ can take any value and thus make the probabilities associated with values of y_i and e_i greater than one or less than zero if $x_i'\beta$ is not contained in the unit interval.

The variance of the random variable e_i is

$$\text{var}(e_i) = \sum_{i=1}^{2} e_i^2 Pr(e_i)$$

$$= (-x_i'\beta)^2(1 - x_i'\beta) + (1 - x_i'\beta)^2(x_i'\beta)$$

$$= (x_i'\beta)(1 - x_i'\beta)$$

$$= (Ey_i)(1 - Ey_i).$$

Thus, if all T observations are written

$$y = X\beta + e$$

$$(A.3)$$

where

$$y = \begin{bmatrix} y_1 \\ y_2 \\ \vdots \\ y_T \end{bmatrix}, \quad X = \begin{bmatrix} 1 & x_{12} & \cdots & x_{1K} \\ 1 & x_{22} & \cdots & x_{2K} \\ \vdots & \vdots & \ddots & \vdots \\ 1 & x_{T2} & \cdots & x_{TK} \end{bmatrix},$$

$$\beta = \begin{bmatrix} \beta_1 \\ \beta_2 \\ \vdots \\ \beta_K \end{bmatrix}, \quad e = \begin{bmatrix} e_1 \\ e_2 \\ \vdots \\ e_T \end{bmatrix},$$

it follows that the covariance matrix of e is

$$\text{cov}\,(e) = Eee' = \Omega, \tag{A.4}$$

where Ω is a diagonal matrix with i-th diagonal element $Ey_i\,(1 - Ey_i)$. Since the error term e_i is heteroscedastic, least squares estimation is inefficient relative to generalized least squares. Recall that for the linear regression model A.3, where X is nonstochastic and of full column rank K, and the vector of random disturbances e has expectation $\mathbf{0}$ and covariance matrix given by equation A.4, the best linear unbiased estimator for β is

$$\tilde{\beta} = (X'\Omega^{-1}X)^{-1}X'\Omega^{-1}y, \tag{A.5}$$

the generalized least squares (GLS) estimator. The variance-covariance matrix of this estimator is

$$E[(\,\tilde{\beta}\, - \beta)(\,\tilde{\beta}\, - \beta)'] = (X'\Omega^{-1}X)^{-1}. \tag{A.6}$$

The variances of this estimator are less than or equal to the variances of any other linear and unbiased estimator for β. Also, since Ω is generally unknown, it must generally be estimated before the GLS estimator can be used. The *feasible* GLS estimator is

$$\tilde{\beta} = (X'\hat{\Omega}^{-1}X)^{-1}X'\hat{\Omega}^{-1}y, \tag{A.7}$$

where $\hat{\Omega}$ is a consistent estimator of Ω. Under some relatively mild assumptions the feasible GLS estimator is *asymptotically* normal with asymptotic covariance matrix given by model A.6.

How generalized least squares estimation is implemented depends upon the nature of the sample data that are available. Often the number of choice outcomes y_i observed for each set of explanatory variables x_i, say n_i, will be just one. That is, we only observe one value of the random variable y_i for each different x_i so that $n_i = 1$. In that case feasible GLS is carried out by estimating model A.1 by least squares. Such an estimation, though inefficient, is consistent. The least squares estimator of β is

$$\hat{\beta} = (X'X)^{-1}X'y. \tag{A.8}$$

This estimator can then be used to construct Ω, a diagonal matrix with elements

$$x_i'\hat{\beta}\,(1 - x_i'\hat{\beta}) = \hat{y}_i(1 - \hat{y}_i). \tag{A.9}$$

Since $\hat{\Omega}$ is diagonal, feasible GLS is easily applied using weighted least squares. That is, multiplication of each observation on the dependent and independent variables by the square root of the reciprocal of model A.9 yields a transformed model, least squares estimation of which produces feasible GLS estimates.

While this estimation procedure is consistent, an obvious difficulty exists. If $x_i'\hat{\beta}$ falls outside the $(0,1)$ interval, the $\hat{\Omega}$ matrix has negative or undefined elements on its diagonal. If this occurs, one must modify $\hat{\Omega}$, either by deleting the observations for which the problem occurs or by setting the value of $x_i'\hat{\beta}$ to, say, .01 or .99, and proceeding. While this does not affect the asymptotic properties of the feasible GLS procedure, it is clearly an awkward position to be in, especially since predictions based on the feasible GLS estimates, $\hat{\tilde{P}}_i = x_i'\hat{\tilde{\beta}}$, may also fall outside the $(0,1)$ interval.

An alternative exists where, for each vector of explanatory variables x_i, repeated observations on y_i are available. That is, let $n_i > 1$ and y_i now be the *number* of occurrences of the event E in n_i choice experiments with the values of the vector of explanatory variables given by x_i. The sample proportion of the number of occurrences of E is then $p_i = y_i/n_i$. Since $E(p_i) = P_i = x_i'\beta$, the model A.1 can be rewritten as

$$P_i = P_i + e_i = x_i'\beta + e_i, \qquad i = 1, \ldots, T, \tag{A.10}$$

where e_i is now the difference between p_i and its expectation P_i. The full set of T observations is then written

$$p = X\beta + e. \tag{A.11}$$

Since the sample proportions p_i are related to the true proportions P_i by

$$p_i = P_i + e_i, \qquad i = 1, \ldots, T,$$

the error term e_i has zero mean and variance $P_i(1 - P_i)/n_i$, the same as the sample proportion based on n_i Bernoulli trials. The covariance matrix of e is

$$\Omega = Eee' = \begin{bmatrix} P_1(1 - P_1)/n_1 & & \\ & P_2(1 - P_2)/n_2 & & 0 \\ & & \ddots & \\ 0 & & & P_T(1 - P_T)/n_T \end{bmatrix}, \tag{A.12}$$

and the appropriate estimator for β in model A.11 is

$$\tilde{\beta} = (X'\Omega^{-1}X)^{-1}X'\Omega^{-1}p, \tag{A.13}$$

the generalized least squares estimator. If the true proportions p_i are not known, then a feasible GLS estimator is

$$\hat{\tilde{\beta}} = (X'\hat{\Omega}^{-1}X)^{-1}X'\hat{\Omega}^{-1}p, \tag{A.14}$$

where the diagonal elements of $\hat{\Omega}$ are $\hat{p}_i(1 - \hat{p}_i)/n_i$, and $\hat{p}_i$ is a suitable consistent estimate of P_i. One alternative is to use $\hat{p}_i = p_i$, the sample proportion. This alternative has the advantage of simplicity and of the fact that p_i falls in the interval $[0,1]$. This makes "adjustment" of the elements of $\hat{\Omega}$ unnecessary unless $\hat{p}_i = 0$ or 1. Another alternative is to let $\hat{p}_i = x_i'\hat{\beta}$ where $\hat{\beta} = (X'X)^{-1}X'p$. Asymptotically the choice does not matter, since $\sqrt{T}(\tilde{\beta} - \beta)$ and $\sqrt{T}(\beta - \beta)$ have the same asymptotic distributions under some general conditions. However, since the feasible GLS predictor takes into account the error covariance matrix Ω, it may be advocated in small samples.

Unfortunately, one must still face the difficulty that the predictor obtained from feasible GLS estimation can fall outside the zero–one interval. To ensure that the predicted proportion of successes will fall within the unit interval, at least over a range of x_i of interest, one may employ inequality restrictions of the form $0 \le x_i'\beta \le 1$ (see Judge et al. [1980, ch. 14] for further details).

As a practical matter the number of repetitions n_i must be large enough so that the sample proportion p_i is a reliable estimate of the probability P_i. On most cases this means that n_i must be at least five or six for the model A.11 to be used effectively.

The difficulty with the *linear probability model* $P_i = x_i'\beta$ is that while $x_i'\beta$ can take any value, unless the values x_i are restricted, P_i must fall in the interval [0,1]. The situation is illustrated in figure A.1 for the case when $x_i'\beta = \beta_1 + \beta_2 x_{i2}$. While the linearity assumption may be appropriate over a range of values of the explanatory variable, it is certainly not appropriate for either extremely large or small values. As an alternative to the linear probability model, the probabilities P_i may be assumed to be a nonlinear function of the explanatory variables. In the next sections two particular nonlinear probability models are discussed, first when repeated observations are available and feasible GLS can be applied, and second when n_i is small and maximum likelihood estimation must be used.

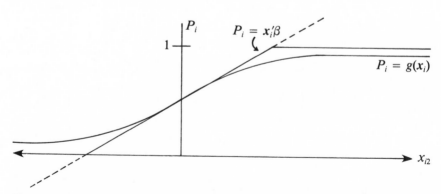

Figure A.1.   Linear and Nonlinear Probability Models

FEASIBLE GLS ESTIMATION OF PROBIT
AND LOGIT MODELS

Two choices of the nonlinear function $P_i = g(x_i)$ are the Cumulative Density Functions (CDFs) of normal and logistic random variables. The former gives rise to the probit model and the latter to the logit model. We may think of the probit model arising as follows. The event E is an action taken by an individual decisionmaker if its expected utility is high enough. What "high enough" is, of course, depends on the individual. Then let $I_i = x_i'\beta$ be a latent index variable — that is, linear in β such that the larger the index variable, the greater the probability of the event E in question occurring. Since that probability must fall between zero and one, the monotonic relationship between I_i and $PR[E \mid I_i]$ must assume the general form of a cumulative density function as shown in figure A.1. Note that we are assuming all individuals weight the explanatory factors x_i identically — that is, the β vector is constant across all individuals, and of all the individuals faced with a particular $x_i'\beta$, some will choose event E and others will choose not-E because of personal preferences.

The following argument for the choice of a normal CDF is often made: Each individual makes a choice between E and not-E by comparing the value of I_i to some threshold level, say I^*, so that if $I_i \geq I^*$, then E occurs. For each individual the value of the threshold I^* is determined by many independent factors and thus can be assumed normally distributed by the central limit theorem. Therefore

$$P_i = Pr(E \mid I_i) = Pr(I_* \leq I_i) = F(I_i) = F(x_i'\beta), \qquad (A.15)$$

where $F(\cdot)$ is the value of the standard normal CDF evaluated at the argument.

A frequently used alternative to the probit model is the logit model. The logit model is based on the logistic CDF and

$$P_i = Pr(I_* \leq x_i'\beta) = \frac{1}{1 + \exp(-x_i'\beta)}, \qquad -\infty < x_i'\beta < \infty. \qquad (A.16)$$

This CDF closely approximates that of a normal random variable and has some convenient properties.

Estimation of the resulting models may be carried out by feasible GLS if several observations are available on each individual — that is, several choice decisions are observed for each observation vector x_i, or maximum likelihood estimation, which is applicable whether repeated observations are available or not.

Feasible GLS Estimation of the Probit Model

Assume that for each vector x_i there are $n_i > 1$ observations and y_i of those resulted in event E. Thus, the sample proportion p_i is $p_i = y_i/n_i$ and is related to the true proportion p_i by

$$p_i = P_i + e_i, \tag{A.17}$$

where $E(e_i) = 0$ and $\text{var}(e_i) = P_i(1 - P_i)/n_i$, the latter following directly from the assumption that the sample proportion p_i is based on n_i independent Bernoulli trials.

The discussion above implies that

$$Pr(E \mid I_i) = P_i = \int_{-\infty}^{I_i} \frac{1}{\sqrt{2\pi}} e^{-\frac{t^2}{2}} \, dt = F(I_i). \tag{A.18}$$

Following Zellner and Lee (1965), we note that

$$F^{-1}(p_i) = F^{-1}(P_i + e_i), \tag{A.19}$$

where $F^{-1}(\cdot)$ is the inverse of the standard normal CDF. Expanding $F^{-1}(P_i + e_i)$ by a Taylor's series about P_i, we obtain

$$F^{-1}(p_i) = F^{-1}(P_i) + e_i \frac{dF^{-1}(P_i)}{dP_i} + R_i. \tag{A.20}$$

Since F is monotonic,

$$\frac{dF^{-1}(P_i)}{dP_i} = \frac{1}{\dfrac{dF(P_i)}{dP_i}} = \frac{1}{f(P_i)}, \tag{A.21}$$

where $f(P_i)$ is the value of the standard normal density evaluated at P_i, and R_i is a remainder that goes to zero in probability as $n_i \to \infty$. Therefore,

$$F^{-1}(p_i) \cong F^{-1}(P_i) + \frac{e_i}{f(P_i)},$$

or

$$v_i = x_i'\beta + u_i, \qquad i = 1, \dots, T, \tag{A.22}$$

where $v_i = F^{-1}(p_i)$ is the "observed" probit, and the random disturbance u_i has $E(u_i) = 0$ and

$$\text{var}(u_i) = \frac{P_i(1 - P_i)}{n_i[f(P_i)]^2}. \tag{A.23}$$

If model A.22 is written as

$$v = X\beta + u,\tag{A.24}$$

the appropriate estimator for β is

$$\tilde{\beta} = (X'\Omega^{-1}X)^{-1}X'\Omega^{-1}v,\tag{A.25}$$

where Ω is a diagonal matrix whose i-th diagonal element is given in A.23. Since Ω is unknown, a feasible GLS estimator is

$$\tilde{\beta} = (X'\hat{\Omega}^{-1}X)^{-1}X'\hat{\Omega}^{-1}v,\tag{A.26}$$

where $\hat{\Omega}$ is based on estimates of P_i, using the sample proportion, the least squares predictions $\hat{p} = X(X'X)^{-1}X'p$, the predictions from the linear probability model, or predictions based on least squares estimation of β in model A.21 and obtained from

$$\tilde{p}_i = \int_{-\infty}^{v_i} f(t)dt,$$

where $\hat{v}_i = x_i'(X'X)^{-1}X'v$ and $f(t)$ is a $N(0,1)$ pdf. The advantage of this latter approach is, of course, that not only are the $\tilde{p}_i$ confined to the $[0,1]$ interval; they are also based on the information provided by the structure A.24.

Since the remainder R_i in model A.20 vanishes in probability, the usual results of feasible generalized least squares hold. That is, the FGLS estimators of model A.21 are consistent and have an asymptotic normal distribution. Therefore, the usual tests of hypotheses can be based on the consistent estimate $(X'\hat{\Omega}^{-1}X)^{-1}$.

Feasible GLS Estimation of the Logit Model

Again assuming that the sample and true proportions are related by

$$p_i = P_i + e_i,$$

then the "odds ratio" is

$$\frac{p_i}{1 - p_i} = \frac{P_i + e_i}{1 - P_i - e_i} = \frac{P_i}{1 - P_i} \cdot \frac{1 + (e_i/P_i)}{1 - (e_i/(1 - P_i))}$$

and the "log-odds" is

$$\ln \frac{p_i}{1 - P_i} = \ln \frac{P_i}{1 - P_i} + \ln\left[1 + \frac{e_i}{P_i}\right] - \ln\left[1 - \frac{e_i}{1 - P_i}\right].$$

Expanding the last two terms about e_i/P_i and $e_i/(1 - P_i)$, respectively, and deleting higher order terms gives

$$\ln \frac{p_i}{1 - p_i} \cong \ln \frac{P_i}{1 - P_i} + \frac{e_i}{P_i} + \frac{e_i}{(1 - P_i)}$$

$$= x_i'\beta + \frac{e_i}{P_i(1 - P_i)} \qquad\qquad (A.27)$$

since $\ln (P_i/(1 - P_i)) = x_i'\beta$ if the logistic structure A.16 is placed on P_i. The model A.27 can be written

$$v_i = x_i'\beta + e_i, \qquad i = 1, \ldots, T, \qquad\qquad (A.28)$$

where $v_i = \ln(p_i/(1 - p_i))$ is called the "observed logit" and $Eu_i = 0$, var $(u_i) = 1/[n_i P_i(1 - P_i)]$. In matrix notation this model is

$$v = X\beta + u, \qquad\qquad (A.29)$$

and the appropriate GLS estimator is

$$\tilde{\beta} = (X'\Omega^{-1}X)^{-1}X'\Omega^{-1}v,$$

where the covariance matrix Ω is diagonal with diagonal elements $1/[n_i P_i(1 - P_i)]$. Once again, since Ω is unknown, the appropriate feasible GLS estimator is

$$\tilde{\tilde{\beta}} = (X'\hat{\Omega}^{-1}X)^{-1}X'\hat{\Omega}^{-1}v, \qquad\qquad (A.30)$$

where $\hat{\Omega}$ is based on estimates of P_i. Candidates for these estimators range from using the sample proportion p_i to using predictions from the linear probability model or predictions based on least squares estimation of model A.29 and computing

$$\hat{p}_i = 1/[1 + \exp(-\hat{v}_i)],$$

where $\hat{v}_i = x_i'(X'X)^{-1}X'v$.

Again the usual results of feasible generalized least squares hold — namely, they are consistent and have an asymptotic normal distribution. Therefore, the usual tests of hypotheses can be based on the consistent estimate $(X'\hat{\Omega}^{-1}X)^{-1}$. The advantage of the logit model over probit is that the inverse of the normal CDF need not be calculated. This is no longer a major consideration given modern computer software.

An Interpretive Note

Finally, a note on the interpretation of the estimated coefficients in logit and probit models. Estimated coefficients do not indicate the increase in the

probability of the event occurring given a one-unit increase in the corresponding independent variable. Rather, the coefficients reflect the effect of a
change in an independent variable upon $F^{-1}(P_i)$ for the probit model and
upon $\ln[P_i/(1 - P_i)]$ for the logit model. In both cases the amount of the increase in the probability depends upon the original probability and thus
upon the initial values of all the independent variables and their coefficients.
This is true since $P_i = F(x_i'\beta)$ and $(\partial P_i)/(\partial x_{ij}) = f(x_i'\beta)\beta_j$, where $f(\cdot)$ is the *pdf*
associated with $F(\cdot)$. For the logit model

$$\frac{\partial P_i}{\partial x_{ij}} = \left[\frac{\exp(-x_i'\beta)}{[1 + \exp(-x_i'\beta)]^2}\right] \cdot \beta_j,$$

and for the probit model

$$\frac{\partial P_i}{\partial x_{ij}} = \frac{\partial}{\partial x_{ij}} \int_{-\infty}^{x_i'\beta} \frac{1}{\sqrt{2\pi}} \exp(-\frac{1}{2}t^2)\, dt$$

$$= \frac{1}{\sqrt{2\pi}} \exp[-\frac{1}{2}(x_i'\beta)^2] \cdot \beta_j.$$

Having examined binary dependent variable models when repeated observations are available, we now consider the binary choice model where only one
or a few observations are available on each choice maker.

MAXIMUM LIKELIHOOD ESTIMATION OF
LOGIT AND PROBIT MODELS

When the number of repeated observations on the choice experiment n_i is
small and P_i cannot be reliably estimated using the sample proportion, maximum likelihood estimation of the logit and probit models can be carried
out. If P_i is the probability that the event E occurs on the i-th trial of the experiment, the random variable y_i, which is one if the event occurs but zero
otherwise, has probability function.

$y_i = 1$ with probability P_i

$y_i = 0$ with probability $1 - P_i$.   (A.31)

Consequently, if T observations are available, the likelihood function is

$$L = \prod_{i=1}^{T} P_i^{y_i}(1 - P_i)^{1 - y_i}.$$ (A.32)

The logit or probit model arises when P_i is specified to be given by the logistic or normal CDF evaluated at $x_i'\beta$. If $F(x_i'\beta)$ denotes either of the CDFs evaluated at $x_i'\beta$, the likelihood function for both models is

$$L = \prod_{i=1}^{T} [F(x_i'\beta)]^{y_i} [1 - F(x_i'\beta)]^{1-y_i}, \tag{A.33}$$

and the log-likelihood function is

$$\ln L = \sum_{i=1}^{T} y_i \ln [F(x_i'\beta)] + (1 - y_i) \ln [1 - F(x_i'\beta)]. \tag{A.34}$$

Whether $F(\cdot)$ is chosen to be the logistic or standard normal CDF, the first-order conditions for a maximum will be nonlinear, so maximum likelihood estimates must be obtained numerically.

One popular computational algorithm for maximum likelihood problems is the Newton-Raphson method. As we do in the case of other iterative techniques, we are trying to find a sequence of vectors $\tilde{\beta}_1, \tilde{\beta}_2, \ldots, \tilde{\beta}_N$ so that $\tilde{\beta}_N$ approximately maximizes the log-likelihood function $\ln L(\beta)$. Starting from some initial vector $\tilde{\beta}_1$, each of the following elements in the sequence is based on the preceding one. Specifically, if $\tilde{\beta}_n$ is the n-th round vector, then

$$\tilde{\beta}_{n+1} = \tilde{\beta}_n + \phi_n,$$

where the vector ϕ_n is called a *step*. The Newton-Raphson method is based on a Taylor's series approximation to $\ln L(\beta)$, given by

$$\ln L(\beta) = \ln L(\tilde{\beta}_n) + \gamma_n'(\beta - \tilde{\beta}_n) + \tfrac{1}{2}(\beta - \tilde{\beta}_n)' H_n(\beta - \tilde{\beta}_n), \tag{A.35}$$

where $\gamma_n = \partial \ln L(\beta)/\partial\beta$ is the gradient vector and

$$H_n = \partial^2 \ln L(\beta)/\partial\beta\partial\beta' \tag{A.36}$$

is the Hessian matrix of second partials, both evaluated at $\tilde{\beta}_n$. The first-order conditions for a maximum of the right-hand side are

$$\gamma_n + H_n(\beta - \tilde{\beta}_n) = \mathbf{0}$$

or

$$\beta = \tilde{\beta}_n - H_n^{-1}\gamma_n. \tag{A.37}$$

Hence, if $\ln L(\beta)$ is quadratic, the equality in model A.35 is exact, and the maximum will be reached in one step given by model A.37. If $\ln L(\beta)$ is not quadratic, expression A.37 may be used iteratively as

$$\tilde{\beta}_{n+1} = \tilde{\beta}_n - H_n^{-1}\gamma_n \tag{A.38}$$

so that the step $\phi_n = -H_n^{-1}\gamma_n$. Equation A.38 is the recursive formula for the method of Newton. It is especially convenient to use since we know that under some regularity conditions, the maximum likelihood estimator, say β^*, is consistent and asymptotically normal with mean β and asymptotic covariance matrix

$$- \left[E \frac{\partial^2 \ln L(\beta)}{\partial \beta \partial \beta'} \right]^{-1},$$

which is the Cramer-Rao lower bound evaluated at the true parameter vector. Furthermore, if β^* is a sufficient statistic (it will be for the cases we consider), then the asymptotic covariance matrix is

$$- \left[\frac{\partial^2 \ln L(\beta)}{\partial \beta \partial \beta'} \right]^{-1}, \tag{A.39}$$

which is just $-H_n^{-1}$. For practical purposes model A.39 is simply evaluated at the maximum likelihood estimate β^*.

Consequently, the Newton-Raphson iterative procedure for maximizing a nonlinear objective function leads to the recursive relation

$$\tilde{\beta}_{n+1} = \tilde{\beta}_n - \left[\frac{\partial^2 \ln L}{\partial \beta \partial \beta'} \right]^{-1}_{\beta = \tilde{\beta}n} \cdot \left[\frac{\partial \ln L}{\partial \beta} \right]_{\beta = \tilde{\beta}_n}, \tag{A.40}$$

where $\tilde{\beta}_n$ is the n-th round estimate, and the matrix of second partials and the gradient vector are evaluated at the n-th round estimate. For finite samples, the asymptotic distribution of β^* can be approximated by

$$N(\beta, \; - \left[\frac{\partial^2 \ln L}{\partial \beta \partial \beta'} \right]^{-1}_{\beta = \beta^*}).$$

Thus, for optimization to be carried out, the first and second derivatives of the log-likelihood function are required. While these derivatives could be approximated numerically, there is no reason to do so for the logit and probit models since they are quite tractable analytically. For the logit model $P_i = F(x_i'\beta)$, where

$$F(t) = \frac{1}{1 + e^{-t}} \tag{A.41}$$

and

$$f(t) = \frac{e^{-t}}{(1 + e^{-t})^2}, \tag{A.42}$$

also note that

$$1 - F(t) = \frac{e^{-t}}{1 + e^{-t}} = F(-t), \tag{A.43}$$

$$\frac{f(t)}{F(t)} = 1 - F(t), \tag{A.44}$$

and

$$f'(t) = -f(t) \cdot F(t) \cdot (1 - e^{-t}). \tag{A.45}$$

Using the definitions A.41 and A.42 and the relations A.43 to A.45, it is not difficult to show that for the logit model

$$\frac{\partial \ln L}{\partial \beta} = \sum_{i=1}^{T} y_i \frac{1}{1 + \exp(x_i'\beta)} x_i - \sum_{i=1}^{T} (1-y_i) \frac{1}{1 + \exp(-x_i'\beta)} \cdot x_i$$
$$= \sum_{i=1}^{T} [y_i F(-x_i'\beta) - (1 - y_i)F(x_i'\beta)]x_i \tag{A.46}$$

and

$$\frac{\partial^2 \ln L}{\partial \beta \partial \beta'} = -\sum_{i=1}^{T} \frac{\exp(-x_i'\beta)}{[1 + \exp(-x_i'\beta)]^2} \cdot x_i x_i'$$
$$= -\sum_{i=1}^{T} f(x_i'\beta) x_i x_i'. \tag{A.47}$$

For the probit model $P_i = F(x_i'\beta)$, where

$$f(t) = \frac{1}{\sqrt{2\pi}} \exp(-\tfrac{1}{2}t^2) \tag{A.48}$$

and

$$F(t) = \int_{-\infty}^{t} f(v)dv, \tag{A.49}$$

also note that

$$f'(t) = -t \cdot f(t) \tag{A.50}$$

and

$$F(-t) = 1 - F(t). \tag{A.51}$$

Then

$$\frac{\partial \ln L}{\partial \beta} = \sum_{i=1}^{T} \left[y_i \frac{f(x_i'\beta)}{F(x_i'\beta)} - (1-y_i) \frac{f(x_i'\beta)}{1 - F(x_i'\beta)} \right] x_i \tag{A.52}$$

and

$$\frac{\partial^2 \ln L}{\partial \beta \partial \beta'} = -\sum_{i=1}^{T} f(x_i'\beta) \left[y_i \cdot \frac{f(x_i'\beta) + (x_i'\beta)F(x_i'\beta)}{[F(x_i'\beta)]^2} \right.$$

$$+ (1 - y_i) \frac{f(x_i'\beta) - (x_i'\beta)(1 - F(x_i'\beta))}{[1 - F(x_i'\beta)]^2} \Bigg] \cdot x_i x_i'. \tag{A.53}$$

Using these derivatives and the recursion relation A.40, we can obtain maximum likelihood estimates given some initial estimates $\tilde{\beta}_1$. For probit and logit models the choice of the initial estimates does not matter since it can be shown (see Dhrymes 1978, pp. 344–47) that for both of these models the matrix of second partials $\partial^2 \ln L / \partial \beta \partial \beta'$ is negative definite for *all* values of β. Consequently, the Newton-Raphson procedure will converge, ultimately, to the unique maximum likelihood estimates regardless of the initial estimates. Computationally, of course, the choice does matter since the better the initial estimates, the fewer iterations must be carried out to attain the maximum of the likelihood function. While several alternatives for initial estimates exist, one can simply use the least squares estimates of β obtained by regressing y_i on the explanatory variables.

The interpretation and evaluation of these models deserves some comment. First, the earlier comments about the interpretation of the estimated coefficients still hold. Specifically, the estimated coefficients do not determine the change in the probability of the even E occurring given a one-unit change in an explanatory variable. Rather, those partial derivatives are

$$\frac{\partial P_i}{\partial x_{ij}} = f(x_i'\beta) \cdot \beta_j,$$

where $f(\cdot)$ is the appropriate *pdf*. Thus while the sign of the coefficient does indicate the *direction* of the change, the magnitude depends upon $f(x_i'\beta)$, which of course reflects the *steepness* of the CDF at $x_i'\beta$. Naturally, the steeper the CDF, the greater the impact of a change in the value of an explanatory variable will be.

Second, usual tests about individual coefficients and confidence intervals can be constructed from the estimate of the asymptotic covariance matrix, the inverse of minus one times matrix of second partials evaluated at the maximum likelihood estimates and using the asymptotic normality of the maximum likelihood estimator. Third, tests of general linear hypotheses $H\beta = h$ can be constructed through use, for example, of the likelihood ratio test. The hypotheses $\beta_2 = \beta_3 = \ldots = \beta_K = 0$ can be easily carried out through the likelihood ratio procedure since the value of the log-likelihood function under the hypothesis is easily attained analytically. If n is the number of successes ($y_i = 1$) observed in the T observations, then for both the logit and the probit models the maximum value of the log-likelihood function under the null hypothesis is

$$\ln L(\hat{\omega}) = n \ln \left(\frac{n}{T}\right) + (T - n) \ln \left(\frac{T - n}{T}\right).$$

Consequently, if the hypothesis is true, then asymptotically

$$-2 \ln \lambda = -2[\ln L(\hat{\omega}) - \ln L(\hat{\Omega})]$$

has a $\chi^2_{(K-1)}$ distribution, where $\ln L(\hat{\Omega})$ is the value of the log-likelihood function evaluated at β^*. Acceptance of this hypothesis would, of course, imply that none of the explanatory variables has any effect on the probability of E occurring. In that case the probability that $y_i = 1$ is estimated to be $P_i = n/T$, which is simply the sample proportion. A related summary measure that is often reported is the Pseudo-R^2, defined as

$$\varrho^2 = 1 - \frac{\ln L(\hat{\Omega})}{\ln L(\omega)}.$$

This measure is 1 when the model is a perfect predictor, in the sense that $\hat{P}_i = F(x_i'\tilde{\beta}) = 1$ when $y_i = 1$ and $\hat{P}_i = 0$ when $y_i = 0$, and is 0 when $\ln L(\hat{\Omega}) = \ln L(\hat{\omega})$. Between these limits the value of ϱ^2 has no obvious intuitive meaning. However, Hauser (1977) shows that ϱ^2 can be given meaning in an information theoretic context. Specifically, ϱ^2 measures the percent of the "uncertainty" in the data explained by the empirical results. See Judge et al. (1980, pp. 602–05) for further discussion.

Finally, logit and probit models might be useful as an alternative to discriminant analysis for classifying individuals into one population or another. Specifically, if $\hat{P}_i \geq 0.5$ in a set of characteristics, x_i may be asserted to "predict" that $y_i = 1$. See Press and Wilson (1978) for a discussion of the relation between discrimination based on logistic models and a discriminant function. However, from a summary point of view it is frequently worthwhile to report the in-sample predictive success of the model — in particular, the number of "correct" predictions, where a prediction is correct when $\hat{P}_i \geq 0.5$ and $y_i = 1$ or $\hat{P}_i < 0.5$ and $y_i = 0$. It is an interesting feature of the logit model that the predicted share of occurrence of the event E — that is, the number of times $\hat{P}_i \geq 0.5$ over T — is equal to the actual share n/T.

SIMULTANEOUS EQUATIONS ESTIMATION WHEN SOME ENDOGENOUS VARIABLES ARE BINARY

In this section we consider an extension by Heckman (1978) of usual simultaneous equations models to the case where some endogenous variables are discrete. The models rely on the notion that discrete endogenous variables are generated by continuous latent (unobservable) variables crossing thresholds. Following Heckman, we will consider a two-equation system that illustrates all the relevant points. Let y_{1i}^* and y_{2i}^* be continuous latent random variables; the simultaneous equation system be

$$y_{1i}^* = X_{1i}\alpha_1 + d_i\beta_1 + y_{2i}^*\gamma_1 + u_{1i}$$

$$y_{2i}^* = X_{2i}\alpha_2 + d_i\beta_2 + y_{1i}^*\gamma_2 + u_{2i} \tag{A.54}$$

where the dummy variable d_i is defined by

$$d_i = 1 \qquad \text{if } y_{2i}^* > 0,$$

$$d_i = 0 \qquad \text{otherwise;} \tag{A.55}$$

and the error terms have a joint normal density with means zero, variances σ_{11} and σ_{22}, and covariance σ_{12}. The vectors X_{1j} and X_{2j} are $(1 \times K_1)$ and $(2 \times K_2)$ vectors of exogenous variables. It is further assumed that if y_{1j}^* and y_{2j}^* are observed and $\beta_1 = \beta_2 = 0$, then the structural equations are identified.

Note that the model is cast in terms of latent variables y_{1j}^* and y_{2j}^* that may or may not be observed directly. Even if y_{2i}^* is never observed, the event $y_{2i}^* > 0$ is observed, and its occurrence is indicated by setting the dummy variable, d_i, to one. Second, note that when $y_{2i}^* > 0$, the structural equations are shifted by an amount β_1 and β_2, respectively. As an example of the use of such a model, let y_{1j}^* be the measured income of blacks in state i while y_{2j}^* is an unmeasured variable that reflects the state's population sentiment toward blacks. If the sentiment is sufficiently high ($y_{2i}^* > 0$), the state may enact antidiscrimination legislation; the presence of such legislation in state i is denoted by the dummy variable d_i taking the value one. In the first equation both sentiment and the presence of legislation are assumed to affect measured income. The sentiment acts in a continuous fashion, and the legislation effect is discrete. An important question is whether the measured effect of legislation is due to the genuine effect of legislation (β_1) or to the contaminating effect — namely, that the presence of favorable legislation is a proxy for the presence of favorable sentiment, which would lead to higher income for blacks in any event (γ_1). These effects can be consistently estimated through use of the techniques described in the following material.

Estimation of the parameters in the equation system can be consistently carried out in a variety of ways. The best estimates are obtained by maximum likelihood estimation, but these estimates are difficult to obtain. Instead we describe a two-step method that does yield consistent estimates of the structural parameters. First, the structural equations can be rewritten in a partially reduced form as

$$y_{1i} = X_{1i}\Pi_{11} + X_{2i}\Pi_{12} + d_i\Pi_{13} + V_{1i}$$

$$y_{2i}^* = X_{1i}\Pi_{21} + X_{2i}\Pi_{22} + d_i\Pi_{23} + V_{2i},$$

where exogenous variables that appear in both structural equations appear here in either X_{1i} or X_{2i} but not in both. Note that we are assuming that y_{1i} is observed, so that it is no longer a latent variable. The assumptions on the reduced-form error terms are that each has expectation zero, variances w_{11} and w_{22}, and contemporaneous covariance w_{12}. Assume that the conditional probability that d_i is one, given X_{1i} and X_{2i}, is P_i. Then the reduced forms can be written

$$y_{1i} = X_{1i}\Pi_{11} + X_{2i}\Pi_{12} + P_i\Pi_{13} + V_{1i} + (d_i - P_i)\Pi_{13}$$

$$y_{2i}^* = X_{1i}\Pi_{21} + X_{2i}\Pi_{22} + P_i\Pi_{23} + V_{2i} + (d_i - P_i)\Pi_{23}.$$

Heckman shows that in order for a structural model to exist, it must be true that

$$\Pi_{23} = \gamma_2\beta_1 + \beta_2 = 0.$$

This assumption rules out the possibility of any structural shift in the reduced-form equation that determines the probability of a shift. Consequently, the reduced form we must work with is

$$y_{1i} = X_{1i}\Pi_{11} + X_{2i}\Pi_{12} + P_i\Pi_{13} + V_{1i} + (d_i - P_i)\Pi_{13} \tag{A.56}$$

$$y_{2i}^* = X_{1i}\Pi_{21} + X_{2i}\Pi_{22} + V_{2i}. \tag{A.57}$$

Estimation of model A.57 is a probit problem, and its estimation yields estimates of the normalized parameters and $\Pi_{22}^* = \Pi_{22}/(w_{22})^{1/2}$, which can be used to estimate the conditional probability of the event that $d_i = 1$. Specifically,

$$\hat{P}_i = F(X_{1i}\hat{\Pi}_{21}^* + X_{2i}\hat{\Pi}_{22}^*), \tag{A.58}$$

where $F(\cdot)$ is the CDF of a standard normal density evaluated at the argument. Furthermore, even though y_{2i}^* is unobservable, we can use the probit estimates to predict its normalized conditional mean as

$$\frac{\hat{y}_{2i}}{w_{22}^{1/2}} = X_{1i}\hat{\Pi}_{21}^* + X_{2i}\hat{\Pi}_{22}^*. \tag{A.59}$$

Now replace y_{2i}^* and d_i in the first equation of model A.54 by their estimated expectations to obtain

$$y_{1i} = X_{1i}\alpha_1 + \hat{P}_i\beta_1 + \frac{\hat{y}_{2i}^*}{(w_{22})^{1/2}}\gamma_1^* + u_{1i}^*, \tag{A.60}$$

where u_{1i}^* is a composite error term. The application of least squares to model A.60 yields unique consistent estimators of α_1, β_1, and γ_1^*. Estimation of the second structural equation may be carried out the same way, though the equation must be normalized so that, rather than y_{2i}^*, y_{1i} (which is observed) appears on the left-hand side of the equation. The resulting equation is

$$y_{1i} = \frac{-1}{\gamma_2^*}((X_{2i}\alpha_2^* + \hat{P}_i\beta_2^*) - \frac{\hat{y}_{2i}^*}{w_{22}^{1/2}}) + u_{2i}^*,$$

where again u_{2i}^* is a composite error term and least squares estimators are consistent. It should be noted that the asymptotic variance covariance matrix produced by least squares is not the usual one. While it is possible to obtain the correct standard errors, it is computationally as difficult as maximum likelihood estimation and will not be discussed here.

An interesting special case of the Heckman model occurs when $\gamma_1 = 0$ — that is, when no latent variable occurs in the first equation. Then the estimated reduced-form probability $\hat{P}_i$ may be used as an instrumental variable for d_i. The standard instrumental variable formulas can be used to estimate the structural parameters and the asymptotic covariance matrix of the estimated structural parameters. Recall that in traditional simultaneous equations models, least squares applied to the structural model, with predicted values of the endogenous variable replacing the actual values of the endogenous variables, produces the two-step least squares estimator that is identical to the equivalent instrumental variable estimator. In the model Heckman has proposed, the two-step least squares estimator is not identical to the instrumental variable estimator proposed above because of the dichotomous nature of d_i. In the contribution and margin equations presented earlier in this book, the dichotomous variables on the right-hand side were aggregated into an index. The authors made the reasonable assumption that the resulting instrument was uncorrelated with the error term, so that two-stage least squares estimates, which they report, are not inappropriate. For the voting equations themselves, two-stage least squares was also applied and provided linear probability model–type estimates for these structural equations, which were consistent.

REFERENCES

Abrams, Burton A., and Russell F. Settle. 1978. "The Economic Theory of Regulation and Public Financing of Presidential Elections." *Journal of Political Economy*, April, pp. 245–57.

Alchian, Armen. 1950. "Uncertainty, Evolution, and Economic Theory." *Journal of Political Economy*, June, pp. 211–21.

Alexander, Herbert E., ed. 1979. *Political Finance*. Beverly Hills, Calif.: Sage Publications.

Almanac of American Politics. 1974, 1978. Michael Barone, Grant Ujifusa, and Douglas Matthews, eds. Boston: Gambit.

Amemiya, Takeshi. 1978. "The Estimation of a Simultaneous Equation Generalized Probit Model." *Econometrica* 46:1193–1206.

American Petroleum Institute. 1975. *Annual Statistical Review*. Washington, D.C.

Americans for Democratic Action. Various issues. *ADA World*.

Ashenfelter, Orley, and Stanley Kelley, Jr. 1975. "Determinants of Participation in Presidential Elections." *Journal of Law and Economics* 18 (3):695–733.

Barzel, Yoram, and Eugene Silberberg. 1973. "Is the Act of Voting Rational?" *Public Choice* 16:51–58.

Beck, Nathaniel. 1975. "The Paradox of Minimax Regret." *American Political Science Review* 69 (3):918–19.

Benston, George J. 1977. "An Appraisal of the Costs and Benefits of Government-

Required Disclosure: SEC and FTC Requirements." *Law and Contemporary Problems* 41:30–62.

Borcherding, Thomas E., ed. 1977. *Budgets and Bureaucrats: The Source of Government Growth.* Durham, N.C.: Duke University Press.

Browning, Edgar K. 1975. *Redistribution and the Welfare System.* Washington, D.C.: American Enterprise Institute for Public Policy Research.

Bruce-Briggs, Barry. 1979. *The New Class?* New Brunswick, N.J.: Transaction Books.

Buchanan, James M., and Gordon Tullock. 1962. *The Calculus of Consent.* Ann Arbor: University of Michigan Press.

Chelius, James Robert. 1977. *Workplace Safety and Health.* Washington, D.C.: American Enterprise Institute.

Coase, Ronald. 1960. "The Problem of Social Cost." *Journal of Law and Economics* 3:1–44.

————. 1974. "Economists and Public Policy." In J. Fred Weston, ed., *Large Corporations in a Changing Society.* New York: New York University Press.

Common Cause. 1974. *Campaign Finance Monitoring Project.* Washington, D.C.

Congressional Quarterly, Inc. Various issues. *Congressional Quarterly Almanac.*

Danielsen, Albert L., and Paul H. Rubin. 1977. "An Empirical Investigation of Voting on Energy Issues." *Public Choice* 31 (Fall):121–28.

Davis, Otto A., and John E. Jackson. 1974. "Representative Voting Assemblies and Demands for Redistribution: The Case of Senate Voting on the Family Assistance Plan." In Harold M. Hochman and George E. Peterson, eds., *Redistribution through Public Choice.* New York: Columbia University Press.

Dhrymes, Phoebus J. 1978. *Introductory Econometrics.* New York: Springer-Verlag.

Downs, Anthony. 1957. *An Economic Theory of Democracy.* New York: Harper & Row.

Epstein, Edwin M. 1979. "The Emergence of Political Action Committees." In Alexander, 1979.

Federal Election Commission. 1979. *FEC Reports on Financial Activity 1977–78.* Washington, D.C.

Ferejohn, John A., and Morris P. Fiorina. 1974. "The Paradox of Not Voting: A Decision Theoretic Analysis." *American Political Science Review* 68 (June):525–36.

————. 1975. "Closeness Counts Only in Horseshoes and Dancing." *American Political Science Review* 69 (3):920–25.

Fiorina, Morris P. 1974. *Representatives, Roll Calls, and Constituencies.* Lexington, Mass.: Lexington Books.

Friedman, Milton. 1962. *Capitalism and Freedom.* Chicago: University of Chicago Press.

————, and Rose Friedman. 1980. *Free to Choose.* New York: Harcourt Brace Jovanovich.

Goldberger, Arthur S. 1964. *Econometric Theory.* New York: Wiley.

Hauser, J. 1977. "Testing the Accuracy, Usefulness, and Significance of Probabilistic Choice Models: An Information Theoretic Approach." Discussion Paper

No. 286. Graduate School of Management/Transportation Center, Northwestern University.

Hayek, Friedrich. 1945. "The Use of Knowledge in Society." *American Economic Review* 35:519–30.

———. 1960. *The Constitution of Liberty*. Chicago: University of Chicago Press.

Heckman, James. 1978. "Dummy Endogenous Variables in a Simultaneous Equation System." *Econometrica*. 46:931–60.

Horwitz, Stanley A. 1976. "The Economic Consequences of Political Philosophy." *Economic Inquiry*, March, pp. 81–88.

Jackson, John E. 1974. *Constituencies and Leaders in Congress*. Cambridge, Mass.: Harvard University Press.

Jacobson, Gary C. 1980. *Money in Congressional Elections*. New Haven, Conn.: Yale University Press.

Jarrell, Gregg A. 1978. "The Demand for State Regulation of the Electric Utility Industry." *Journal of Law and Economics* 21:269–95.

Jordan, William A. 1972. "Producer Protection, Prior Market Structure, and the Effects of Government Regulation." *Journal of Law and Economics* 15:151–76.

Judge, George G., et al. 1980. *The Theory and Practice of Econometrics*. New York: Wiley.

Kahn, Alfred E. 1970. *The Economics of Regulation*, 2 vols. New York: Wiley.

Kau, James B., and Paul H. Rubin. 1978. "Voting on Minimum Wages: A Time Series Analysis." *Journal of Political Economy* 86 (2, part 1):337–42.

———. 1979a. "Public Interest Lobbies: Membership and Influence." *Public Choice* 34 (1):45–54.

———. 1979b. "Self-Interest, Ideology, and Logrolling in Congressional Voting." *Journal of Law and Economics* 22 (2):365–84.

Keynes, John Maynard. 1936. *The General Theory of Employment, Interest, and Money*. London: Harcourt, Brace & World.

Kingdon, John W. 1973. *Congressmen's Voting Decisions*. New York: Harper & Row.

Lancaster, Kelvin J. 1966. "A New Approach to Consumer Theory." *Journal of Political Economy* 74:132–57.

Linneman, Peter. 1980. "The Economic Impact of Minimum Wage Laws: A New Look at an Old Question." Working Paper. Center for the Study of the Economy and the State, University of Chicago.

Luenberger, David. 1969. *Optimization by Vector Space Methods*. New York: Wiley.

MacAvoy, Paul W. 1965. *The Economic Effects of Regulation: The Trunk Line Cartels and the Interstate Commerce Commission before 1900*. Cambridge, Mass.: MIT Press.

McCormick, Robert E., and Robert D. Tollison. 1981. *Politicians, Legislation, and the Economy*. Boston: Martinus Nijhoff.

McFarland, Andrew S. 1976. *Public Interest Lobbies: Decision Making on Energy*. Washington, D.C.: American Enterprise Institute.

Matthews, Donald R., and James A. Stimson. 1975. *Yeas and Nays*. New York: Wiley.

Mayer, Lawrence S., and I.J. Good. 1975. "Is Minimax Regret Applicable to Voting Decisions?" *American Political Science Review* 69 (3):916–17.

Moore, Sally Falk. 1978. *Law as Process*. London: Routledge & Kegan Paul.

Mueller, Dennis C. 1979. *Public Choice*. New York: Cambridge University Press.

Nash, John F., Jr. 1950. "Equilibrium Points in N-Person Games." *Proceedings of the National Academy of Sciences* 36:48–49.

Nerlove, Marc, and S. James Press. 1973. *Univariate and Multivariate Log-Linear and Logisitic Models*. R-1306-EDA/NIH, December. Rand Corporation, Santa Monica, Calif.

Nisbet, Robert. 1980. *History of the Idea of Progress*. New York: Basic Books.

Niskanen, William A., Jr. 1971. *Bureaucracy and Representative Government*. Chicago: Aldine.

Nozick, Robert. 1974. *Anarchy, State, and Utopia*. New York: Basic Books.

Olson, Mancur, Jr. 1965. *The Logic of Collective Action*. Cambridge, Mass.: Harvard University Press.

Palda, Kristian S. 1975. "The Effect of Expenditure on Political Success." *Journal of Law and Economics* 18:745–71.

Peltzman, Sam. 1973. "An Evaluation of Consumer Protection Legislation: The 1962 Drug Amendments. *Journal of Political Economy* 81:1049–91.

———. 1975. "The Effects of Automobile Safety Regulation." *Journal of Political Economy* 83:677–725.

———. 1976. "Toward a More General Theory of Regulation." *Journal of Law and Economics* 19 (2):211–40.

Posner, Richard A. 1974. "Taxation by Regulation." *Bell Journal of Economics and Management Science* 5 (2):335–58.

———. 1977. *Economic Analysis of Law*. Boston: Little, Brown.

Press, S. James, and Sandra Wilson. 1978. "Choosing between Logistic Regression and Discriminant Analysis." *Journal of the American Statistical Association* 73:699–705.

Ridker, Ronald G., and John A. Henning. 1967. "The Determinants of Residential Property Values with Special Reference to Air Pollution." *Review of Economics and Statistics* 49 (2):246–57.

Riker, William H. 1962. *The Theory of Political Coalitions*. New Haven, Conn.: Yale University Press.

Rubin, Paul H. 1975. "On the Form of Special Interest Legislation." *Public Choice* 21 (Spring):79–90.

Schmidt, Peter, and Robert P. Strauss. 1975. "Estimation of Models with Jointly Dependent Qualitative Variables: A Simultaneous Logit Approach." *Econometrica*, July, pp. 745–55.

———. 1976. "The Effect of Unions on Earnings and Earnings on Unions: A Mixed Logit Approach." *International Economic Review* 17 (1):204–12.

Schneider, Jerrold E. 1979. *Ideological Coalitions in Congress*. Westport, Conn.: Greenwood Press.

Schumpeter, Joseph A. 1950. *Capitalism, Socialism, and Democracy*. New York: Harper & Row.

Schwert, G. William. 1977. "Public Regulation of National Securities Exchanges: A Test of the Capture Hypothesis." *Bell Journal of Economics* 8:128–50.

Silberman, Jonathan I., and Garey C. Durden. 1976. "Determining Legislative Preferences on the Minimum Wage: An Economic Approach." *Journal of Political Economy* 84 (2):317–29.

Stephens, Stephen V. 1975. "The Paradox of Not Voting: Comment." *American Political Science Review* 69 (3):914–15.

Stigler, George J. 1964. "Public Regulation of the Securities Market." *Journal of Business of the University of Chicago* 37:117–42.

——. 1971. "The Theory of Economic Regulation." *Bell Journal of Economics and Management Science* 2 (1):3–21.

——. 1974. "Free Riders and Collective Action: An Appendix to Theories of Economic Regulation." *Bell Journal of Economics and Management Science* 5 (2):359–65.

——. 1976. "Do Economists Matter?" *Southern Economic Journal* 42 (3):347–54.

——. 1980. "The Economist as Preacher"; "The Ethics of Competition: The Friendly Economists"; "The Ethics of Competition: The Unfriendly Critics." Tanner Lectures given at Harvard University. Published as special papers by the Center for the Study of the Economy and State, University of Chicago.

——, and Clare Friedland. 1962. "What Can Regulators Regulate?: The Case of Electricity." *Journal of Law and Economics* 5:1–16.

Strom, Gerald S. 1975. "On the Apparent Paradox of Participation: A New Proposal." *American Political Science Review* 69 (3):908–13.

Troy, Leo. 1957. *Distribution of Union Membership among the States, 1939 and 1953.* New York: National Bureau of Economic Research.

Tullock, Gordon. 1967. *Towards a Mathematics of Politics.* Ann Arbor: University of Michigan Press.

——. 1975. "The Paradox of Not Voting for Oneself." *American Political Science Review* 69 (3):919–20.

Uri, Noel D., and J. Wilson Mixon, Jr. 1980. "An Economic Analysis of the Determinants of Minimum Wage Voting Behavior." *Journal of Law and Economics* 23:167–77.

U.S. Bureau of the Census. 1977. *Statistical Abstract.* Washington, D.C.: Government Printing Office.

U.S. Bureau of Mines. 1975. *Minerals Yearbook.* Washington, D.C.: Government Printing Office.

U.S. Congress. 1938. *Journal of the House of Representatives.* Washington, D.C.: Government Printing Office.

U.S. Department of Commerce. N.d. *Regional Employment by Industry, 1940–1970.* Washington, D.C.: Government Printing Office.

U.S. Department of Labor. 1975. *Handbook of Labor Statistics.* Washington, D.C.: Government Printing Office.

Viscusi, W. Kip. 1979. "The Impact of Occupational Safety and Health Regulation." *Bell Journal of Economics* 10 (1):117–40.

Wardell, William M., and Louis Lasagna. 1975. *Regulation and Drug Development.*
    Washington, D.C.: American Enterprise Institute.
Weidenbaum, Murray. 1981. *Business, Government, and the Public.* Englewood
    Cliffs, N.J.: Prentice-Hall.
Weisberg, Herbert F. 1978. "Evaluating Theories of Congressional Roll-Call
    Voting." *American Journal of Political Science* 22:554–77.
Willard, Stephen. 1970. *General Topology.* Reading, Mass.: Addison-Wesley.
Wittman, Donald. 1975. "Comment." *Journal of Law and Economics* 18 (3):735–41.
Wold, Herman. 1954. "Casuality and Econometrics." *Econometric* 22 (1):162–77.
Zellner, Arnold, and Tong Hun Lee. 1965. "Joint Estimation of Relationships In-
    volving Discrete Random Variables." *Econometrica* 33:382–94.

INDEX

bies and, 52; and roll call voting, 34, 36. *See also* Democrats

Paternalism, 14, 15

Peltzman, Sam: on cost-benefit calculation, 16; on public choice, 12; on self-interest, 12, 13

Pipefitters Local 562 v. *United States*, 105, 106

Policy making: advocacy and, 26–27; free riding in, 26; influences on, 21–30, 106, 107, 124; intellectuals and, 26–27; Stigler on, 27–28, 30. *See also* Economists, functions of

Political action committees. *See* PACs

Political agents. *See* Agents

Political party. *See* Party

Political process. *See* Voting, citizens'

Political scientists, 12, 25, 26, 31–35, 46

Price controls, wage and, 93

Probability, factors of, 126

Probability models, nonlinear, 131–140

Probit models: as alternative to discriminant analysis, 140; based on CDFs, equation for, 131; estimated coefficients in, interpretation of, 134–135; feasible GLS estimation of, 131, 132–133. *See also* Logit models

Producers, benefits of, 17

Profit maximization, 33

Promarket position, definition of, 21

Public choice: 11–13, 29. *See also* Self-interest

Public Citizen: influence of, 49–53; membership in, and education, 47–48; membership statistics of, 46; party affiliation of, 52. *See also* Common Cause; Public interest lobbies

Public interest lobbies: communication costs of, 47; ideology of, 49; influence of, 45–54; membership of, 46–49; as public good, 49; standard economic theory of, 45. *See also* Common Cause; Public Citizen

Public policy making. *See* Policy making

RADA: in conditional probability model, 77; in logit analysis, 67–76

Rational ignorance. *See* Ignorance

Reaction functions in general equilibrium model, 37

Recursive system, use of, 49–52

Regulation: counterproductive, 10–11; economic, theories of, 10–13, mentioned, 121; effects of, 10–11, 25; gainers and losers of, 12; market failure and, 10, 11; optimal, 10, 11; OSHA, 9, 18; Peltzman on, 12; SEC, 9, 17; Stigler on, 22; useless or harmful, 21–23. *See also* New regulation; Old regulation

Representatives. *See* Congressmen

Roll call voting: changes in, general equilibrium model used to measure influence of contributions on, 115–119; congressmen's use of, 36; consistency of, 60; constituencies and, 32, 34, 35; contributors and, 35, 36–37; cue setters for, 34; as data in general equilibrium model, 83–84; as data about legislation, 31–42; economic analysis of, 31–42; equilibrium approach to, 86; factors of, 36, 56; government employees and, in logit analysis, 75; political science analysis of, 31–35; prediction of, 34; significant variables in, 33–34; studies of, 86; variables in, 93–100; welfare payments and, 61 n. 3

—determinants of: contributions as, 105–124; in general equilibrium model, 45–101; general equilibrium model used to measure, 9–42

—determinants of, voting on minimum wage laws used to measure: analysis of, 55–61; average hourly earnings and, 58; black population and, 57, 58, 60; high-wage workers and, 60;